10TH ANNIVERSARY EDITION

The I ♥ TRADER JOE'S® COLLEGE COOKBOOK

180 Quick and Easy Recipes for Busy (and Broke) College Students

ANDREA LYNN

Published by:
Ulysses Press
PO Box 3440
Berkeley, CA 94703
www.ulyssespress.com

ISBN: 978-1-64604-244-9
Library of Congress Catalog Number: 2021937809

Printed in China

10 9 8 7 6 5 4 3

Acquisitions editor: Ashten Evans
Managing editor: Claire Chun
Project editor: Renee Rutledge
Editor: Kathy Kaiser
Cover artwork: front—books © frescomovie/shutterstock.com, coffee cup © Lilkin/shutterstock
    .com, pasta © Epine/shutterstock.com, beer © Doris Rich/shutterstock.com; back—
    judiswinksphotography.com
Food stylist: Anna Hartman-Kenzler for recipes on pages 22, 27, 30, 39, 42, 48, 57, 62, 67, 73, 74, 80, 87,
    93, 99, 105, 109, 112, 115, 123, 126, 129, 134, 139, 144, 147, 180, 184
Interior photos: see page 196
Production: Yesenia Garcia-Lopez

CONTENTS

INTRODUCTION

Trader Joe's is a mecca of affordable, good-quality, delicious food—perfect for the college student who wants more than just cafeteria meals. With a little creativity and this cookbook in hand, you can transform Trader Joe's ingredients into a mouthwatering array of nibbles and meals.

The purpose of this cookbook is to highlight basic recipes with step-by-step instructions, utilizing the wonder that is Trader Joe's. Take it from someone who's sampled every ingredient the company makes: From packaged snacks to fresh veggies to frozen meals, there's a reason why the chain is so popular—the food is unique and tasty, and they're constantly coming up with new products.

For the new cook, an onslaught of so many ingredients can be overwhelming, but this cookbook was created to work with the limited time and new cooking skills of a college student. From snacks to feed a study group to sandwiches for a lunch on the run to a quick soup on a cold day, this book's got you covered. For dinner, you can use a microwave to whip up delicious dishes from your dorm room, tackle quick pasta recipes and hearty meals, and create special-occasion feasts for friends and family. There are even recipes for brain-boosting foods to help you out during exam weeks, and vegetarian options for when you need a little less meat. And, of course, what cookbook would be complete without a touch of dessert love? When you need a sweet treat in your life, tweak Trader Joe's products for a quick fix.

Chock-full of 180 recipes, all using the best Trader Joe's has to offer, this book makes your job simple. Select a few recipes, head to your local Trader Joe's, and relish in the delicious creativity that comes from combining their ingredients to make a feast.

USING THIS BOOK

SUBSTITUTIONS

One of the greatest things about Trader Joe's is that in one shopping trip you can gather all the ingredients you'll need to make the recipes in this book. But sometimes you'll find that one location doesn't carry a certain item, that your absolute favorite Trader Joe's salsa has suddenly been discontinued, or that something you're craving is only stocked around the holidays. No worries—although the recipes here are all made using many TJ's-specific ingredients, those can easily be substituted with a similar generic item. Or Trader Joe's often has a similar ingredient in stock: Can't find Trader Joe's Misto alla Griglia? See if they have Trader Joe's Grilled Eggplant and Zucchini Mélange. Use the recipes here as guidelines and you'll still be whipping up delicious dishes in no time and getting back to that term paper you've been putting off.

RECIPE ICONS

Whether you're looking for a quick snack to take to class or a heartier meal that you can still make with limited equipment (no stove? no problem!), handy icons accompany each recipe to quickly narrow your options: Microwave Only, One-Pot Cooking, Five-Minute Prep, No Cook, Grab and Go, and Vegetarian/Vegan. No matter what your cooking mood is, there's a recipe to match.

🔲	**meals that can be prepared entirely in a microwave**
🍲	**meals that require just one pot**
⏱	**meals that can be prepared in five minutes or less**
⊡	**meals that require no cooking**
🎒	**meals that are great to take on the go**
🌿	**meals that are vegetarian or vegan**

CHAPTER 1

BREAKFAST

The previous edition of this cookbook didn't have a breakfast chapter, instead spreading breakfast recipes throughout the book. In revamping this book for the 10-year anniversary edition, this was an obvious add-in. Breakfast foods are so convenient and can be eaten any time of the day, whether you've rolled out of bed at noon or are dashing to class much earlier in the morning. From the ever-portable Tortilla, Egg, and Cheese Wrap and Avocado Toast with Everything Bagel Seasoning to brunch-worthy Skillet Chilaquiles and Acai Bowls to trendy Mini Cookie Cereal, you'll find everything you need to start the day with a bang.

ACAI BOWLS

Keeping Trader Joe's acai puree packets and frozen banana chunks in the freezer means an affordable acai bowl is at your disposal any time you want. To turn this into a smoothie, use fresh banana instead of frozen and add ½ cup of liquid, such as milk, juice, or water.

1 packet Trader Joe's Unsweetened Organic Acai Puree

1 peeled banana, sliced and frozen

½ cup Trader Joe's Lowfat Vanilla Bean Yogurt

sliced fresh fruit, as needed, such as kiwi, banana, strawberries, blueberries, pomegranate seeds, etc.

1 tablespoon unsweetened coconut, granola, sliced nuts, or some combination (optional)

Yield: 1 serving
Prep Time: 10 minutes
Cook Time: none

1. Follow the directions for the acai puree packet, holding it under running water to thaw and breaking it into smaller pieces with your hands. (Note: Large pieces will not break up in the blender.)

2. To a blender, add the acai, frozen banana, and yogurt. Puree until smooth, adding just 1 to 2 tablespoons of water if needed to get the mixture to blend.

3. Pour the mixture into a wide bowl. Top with the fruit and additional toppings, if using. Serve immediately.

FRENCH TOAST and SAUSAGE SANDWICHES

This quick and easy sandwich is super simple and deliriously delicious.

4 Trader Joe's Veggie Sausage Patties

1 (12.2-ounce) box Trader Joe's Brioche French Toast

2 tablespoons unsalted butter, cut into pieces

2 tablespoons maple syrup

Yield: 2 sandwiches
Prep Time: 5 minutes
Cook Time: 5 minutes

1. Microwave the sausage patties according to the package directions and cook the French toast in the toaster until golden.

2. In a small bowl, microwave the butter on high until just softened, 5 to 10 seconds. Stir in the maple syrup.

3. Lay half of the toast slices on a cutting board and soak with the maple syrup and butter.

4. Slice the patties in half and place 2 on each of the toast slices. Top with the remaining toast.

CHOCOLATY OVERNIGHT OATS

You'll thank yourself in the morning for making this breakfast the night before. To make this recipe dairy-free, use plant-based milk and yogurt.

1 cup Trader Joe's Oven Toasted Old Fashioned Organic Oats or Trader Joe's Rolled Oats

¾ cup milk

¾ cup plain yogurt

1 tablespoon honey or maple syrup

¼ teaspoon Trader Joe's Ground Cinnamon (optional)

2 tablespoons Trader Joe's Chocolate Hummus

stir-ins, such as fresh fruit, dried fruit, or chopped nuts (optional)

Yield: 2 servings
Prep Time: 5 minutes, plus overnight to refrigerate
Cook Time: none

1. In a medium bowl, combine the oats, milk, yogurt, honey or maple syrup, and cinnamon, if using. If the mixture is too thick to stir, add another 1 to 2 tablespoons of milk.

2. Cover the mixture and refrigerate overnight. Stir the chocolate hummus into the oatmeal. Add the stir-ins, if using, or eat as is.

NUT BUTTER with BANANA SANDWICHES

This is an absolute staple for my breakfast, and I usually make it open-faced. It's easy, healthy, and delicious.

4 slices Trader Joe's Soft 10 Grain Bread, or another type of bread, toasted if desired

Trader Joe's Creamy Almond Butter, Salted or Trader Joe's Mixed Nut Butter, as needed

2 teaspoons honey

1 banana, sliced

Yield: 2 sandwiches
Prep Time: 5 minutes
Cook Time: none

1. Spread 2 slices of bread with almond butter and drizzle with honey.

2. Divide the banana pieces between the slices of bread, and top each one with a second slice.

Note: Leftover Nut Butter with Banana Sandwich? No problem, see page 194.

MINI COOKIE CEREAL

The viral trend of mini cookie cereal is made easy when you start with packaged cookie dough.

½ (16-ounce) package Trader Joe's Chunky Chocolate Chip Cookie Dough

milk or a plant-based milk alternative, as needed

Yield: 2 servings
Prep Time: 15 minutes
Cook Time: 15 minutes

1. Preheat the oven to 325°F. Line a large cookie sheet with foil and coat it with cooking spray.

2. Break off 1 piece of the chocolate chip cookie dough. Cut it into 8 equal pieces, and place the pieces on the cookie sheet. Repeat with the remaining cookie dough pieces.

3. Bake for 12 to 15 minutes, until the cookies are crisp. Let cool completely. Store in an airtight container for 2 to 3 days, or eat immediately by adding the cookies to a bowl and serving with milk or a plant-based milk alternative.

BERRY SHORTCAKE WAFFLES

The crunch of freeze-dried berries offers a nice texture in this easy breakfast. If desired, swap out the freeze-dried berries for ¼ cup of chopped fresh berries.

2 Trader Joe's Multi Grain Toaster Waffles

1 can sweetened light whipped cream, as needed

½ cup Trader Joe's Organic Freeze-Dried Berry Medley, crushed (optional)

Yield: 1 serving
Prep Time: 3 minutes
Cook Time: 1 minute

1. Toast the waffles in a toaster. Place the waffles on a plate and top generously with the whipped cream.

2. Sprinkle the freeze-dried fruit, if using, over the whipped cream. Serve immediately.

SKILLET CHILAQUILES with SCRAMBLED EGGS

A true chilaquiles uses tortillas fried in oil, but this shortcut using chips is equally delicious and much easier. If you can't find the pepita salsa, any smooth salsa will do.

½ (10-ounce) jar Trader Joe's Pepita Salsa (¾ cup)

½ cup water

2 large eggs

5 cups tortilla chips, such as Trader Joe's Veggie and Flaxseed Tortilla Chips

¼ cup Trader Joe's Shredded Sharp Cheddar Cheese

Yield: 2 servings
Prep Time: 5 minutes
Cook Time: 6 minutes

1. In a 10-inch skillet, combine the salsa and water. Heat to a simmer on high. Meanwhile, crack the eggs into a small bowl and beat with a fork.

2. Add the chips to the skillet and gently stir to coat them with the salsa. Reduce the heat to medium-high. Cook for 2 to 3 minutes, stirring constantly with a spatula to coat the chips in salsa. Make a well in the center of the tortilla chips and add the eggs to it. Let them cook for 1 minute undisturbed.

3. Using the spatula, continue to stir the mixture together until the eggs are scrambled and cooked, 1 to 2 minutes. Remove from the heat and stir in the cheese. Serve immediately.

COLD BREW with WHIPPED CREAM and CHOCOLATE SYRUP

This easy cold brew drink looks and tastes as impressive as a Starbucks drink, without breaking the budget.

2 to 4 tablespoons Trader Joe's Instant Cold Brew Coffee

sugar, as needed

1 cup water

milk or cream, as needed

Trader Joe's Organic Midnight Moo Chocolate Syrup, as needed

ice cubes, as needed

1 can sweetened light whipped cream, as needed

Yield: 1 serving
Prep Time: 5 minutes
Cook Time: none

1. To a tall glass, add the instant cold brew coffee and sugar. Add the water, stirring to combine.

2. Stir in the milk or cream and chocolate syrup.

3. Add the ice cubes and top with the whipped cream and more chocolate syrup, if desired.

BACON, EGG, and CHEESE BREAKFAST SANDWICH

Stash the English muffins in the freezer and keep bacon, eggs, and cheese on hand for a microwave breakfast that's good at home or on the go.

1 large egg

⅛ teaspoon kosher salt

⅛ teaspoon freshly ground black pepper

1 slice Trader Joe's Organic American Sliced Cheese

2 strips Trader Joe's Fully Cooked Uncured Bacon

1 Trader Joe's Sourdough English Muffin

2 teaspoons olive oil

Yield: 1 serving
Prep Time: 5 minutes
Cook Time: 5 minutes

1. Crack the egg into a small heatproof bowl. Season with salt and pepper. Whisk the egg with a fork. Microwave the egg in 15-second intervals, stirring each time, until it is almost set, 30 to 45 seconds. Top with the slice of cheese, and microwave 15 seconds more. Let cool slightly.

2. Meanwhile, microwave the bacon according to package directions and toast the English muffin. Drizzle the oil on both halves of the English muffin. Top the bottom half with the egg and bacon; close with the top half of the English muffin and serve.

ULTIMATE BREAKFAST BOOSTING SMOOTHIE

The reasonable price of Trader Joe's nutrition staples, such as flaxseed and hemp seeds, makes them a must-buy. Add them to an energy-boosting morning smoothie.

½ cup low-fat plain yogurt

1 banana

½ cup frozen pineapple tidbits

¼ cup frozen spinach

½ cup low-fat milk or nondairy milk

2 tablespoons Trader Joe's Shelled Hemp Seeds

2 tablespoons Trader Joe's Organic Flaxseed Meal

2 teaspoons Trader Joe's Matcha Green Tea Powder (optional)

3 or 4 ice cubes

Yield: 1 serving
Prep Time: 5 minutes
Cook Time: none

1. To a blender, add the yogurt, banana, pineapple, spinach, low-fat milk or nondairy milk, hemp seeds, flaxseed meal, and green tea powder, if using. Top with the ice cubes.

2. Purée until the pineapple tidbits become incorporated, the ice cubes disappear, and the smoothie is thoroughly blended, 30 seconds to 1 minute.

AVOCADO TOAST with EVERYTHING BAGEL SEASONING

Avocado contains monounsaturated fat (the good kind of fat), which goes hand in hand with better brain activity.

2 slices Trader Joe's Soft 10 Grain Bread

1 avocado, diced (for dicing tips, see page 192)

squeeze of lemon juice (optional)

Trader Joe's Everything But the Bagel Sesame Seasoning, as needed

Yield: 2 pieces
Prep Time: 5 minutes
Cook Time: 1 minute

1. Toast the bread in a toaster. Meanwhile, in a small bowl, mash the avocado with a fork until smooth. Stir in the lemon juice, if using.

2. Spread the avocado onto each piece of toast. Sprinkle with a generous layer of seasoning and serve.

TORTILLA, EGG, and CHEESE WRAP

1 medium egg

⅛ teaspoon kosher salt

⅛ teaspoon freshly ground black pepper

2 tablespoons Trader Joe's Onion & Chive Cream Cheese Spread

1 Trader Joe's Handmade Tortilla

½ teaspoon Trader Joe's Italian Bomba Hot Pepper Sauce (optional)

Yield: 1 serving
Prep Time: 5 minutes
Cook Time: 5 minutes

1. Crack the egg into a small bowl. Add the salt and pepper, and whisk the mixture to combine. Spread a layer of cream cheese onto the tortilla and top it with hot pepper sauce, if using.

2. Coat a medium nonstick pan with cooking spray. Heat on medium and add the egg. Using a spatula, stir the egg and cook for 30 seconds. Top with the tortilla (cream cheese–side down), pressing down fully over the egg mixture. Cook for about 1 minute, until the egg is fully cooked. Using a spatula, flip to warm the other side, 15 to 30 seconds.

3. Transfer the tortilla to a plate and roll up like a wrap. Eat immediately.

ENGLISH CRUMPET with FRUITY CREAM CHEESE

A crumpet has so many fluffy crevices just waiting to be smeared with melted butter or a fruity cream cheese topping. Just as with English muffins, freeze any remaining crumpets and pull them out when you need them.

1 Trader Joe's British Style Crumpet

1 tablespoon any fruit spread, such as Trader Joe's Organic Raspberry Spread or Trader Joe's Organic Watermelon Spread

1 tablespoon Trader Joe's Organic Whipped Cream Cheese

Yield: 1 serving
Prep Time: 5 minutes
Cook Time: 1 minute

1. Toast the crumpet.

2. In a small bowl, stir together the fruit spread and cream cheese until combined. Spread onto the crumpet.

CHAPTER 2

SNACKS & NIBBLES

If you've ever thought, "When will I need to make an appetizer?" then let me ask *you* a question in return: When is there a time an appetizer isn't appropriate? Think of it as food that's low on the commitment scale—fewer ingredients and minimal instructions, all resulting in a smaller quantity of food. I could eat entire meals made straight from the nibbles in this chapter. In fact, I have.

So look at these recipes as a smorgasbord of sorts. When you want something to nibble on while walking to class, go for a recipe like the irresistible Bratwursts in a Blanket. Want to feed a study group coming to your dorm? Try Thai Red Curry Deviled Eggs or Mini Tostadas with Beef Brisket. Maybe you just want a plateful of Stuffed Mushrooms to feast on while cramming for an exam. Or serve up Spicy Boneless Chicken Pieces to cheer on a sports team. These recipes will make snack time much more rewarding than just tearing open the bag of chips you have lying around.

STUFFED MUSHROOMS

By removing the stem from a mushroom, you create a portable vessel to stuff with cheesy goodness.

2 ounces cream cheese

¼ (6-ounce) bag baby spinach

2 tablespoons Trader Joe's Roasted Red Pepper and Artichoke Tapenade

8 ounces white mushrooms

Trader Joe's Grated Parmigiano-Reggiano cheese (optional)

Yield: 4 servings
Prep Time: 10 minutes
Cook Time: 13 minutes

1. Preheat the oven to 450°F. Spray a baking sheet with cooking spray.

2. Place the cream cheese and spinach in a microwave-safe bowl. Microwave on high until the cream cheese has softened, 30 seconds to 1 minute. Stir the spinach and cream cheese together, then stir in the tapenade until combined.

3. Remove the stems from the mushrooms and use a wet paper towel to wipe the outside of each mushroom clean. Spoon the mixture into each cavity and arrange the stuffed mushrooms on the prepared baking sheet.

4. Bake until the cheese is bubbly and the mushrooms are cooked, 10 to 12 minutes. Sprinkle with Parmigiano-Reggiano, if desired.

FRIED CHICKPEAS

Whether you call them chickpeas or garbanzo beans, they're still delicious. The crispy fried coating gives way to the smooth softness of the beans in this vegan snack.

¼ cup cornstarch

¼ cup flour

1 teaspoon kosher salt, plus more for sprinkling

1 (15-ounce) can chickpeas, drained

canola oil, as needed

Yield: 4 servings
Prep Time: 5 minutes
Cook Time: 10 minutes

1. Line a plate with a paper towel. In a large bowl, combine the cornstarch, flour, and salt. Working in batches, add the chickpeas to the cornstarch mixture, coating thoroughly.

2. Toss the coated chickpeas into a strainer, shaking to remove excess coating.

3. In a large, deep pan, heat 1 inch of oil over high heat until shimmering.

4. When the oil is hot, add half the chickpeas and cook until crisp, 3 to 4 minutes. Transfer with a slotted spoon onto the prepared plate. Repeat with the remaining chickpeas. Sprinkle salt over the fried chickpeas.

OLIVE FOCACCIA

The great thing about tapenade is that all the work's been done for you and it can be used in many ways. Here, it's merged with pizza dough for an easy vegan focaccia.

flour, as needed

1 ball Trader Joe's pizza dough, at room temperature

1 tablespoon olive oil, plus more as needed

3 tablespoons Trader Joe's Olive Tapenade Spread, divided

2 Roma tomatoes, thinly sliced lengthwise

½ teaspoon kosher salt

Yield: 4 servings
Prep Time: 10 minutes
Cook Time: 30 minutes

1. Preheat the oven to 400°F.

2. Sprinkle 1 to 2 tablespoons of flour onto a cutting board. Place the pizza dough on the cutting board and gently knead it. Then gently stretch the dough out with your fingers.

3. In an 8 x 12-inch glass baking dish, combine the oil and 1 tablespoon of olive tapenade, and spread the mixture around the bottom of the dish.

4. Spread the pizza dough over the olive oil and tapenade, pressing the dough down into the bottom of the dish. Use your fingers to punch tiny indentations into the top of the dough.

5. Spread the remaining tapenade on top, then layer tomato slices over the top of the dough and sprinkle with the salt. Bake until the focaccia is puffy and golden, 25 to 30 minutes. Drizzle with olive oil and cut into pieces.

GUACAMOLE with TOMATILLOS

For this vegan guacamole, the avocado is paired with the tangy tomatillos in the salsa verde.

juice of ½ lime

1 scallion, chopped

2 tablespoons Trader Joe's Organic Tomatillo and Roasted Yellow Chili Salsa

½ jalapeño, seeds and ribs removed, minced (optional)

½ teaspoon kosher salt

2 avocados, diced (for tips on dicing, see page 192)

tortillas or chips

Yield: 4 servings
Prep Time: 5 minutes
Cook Time: none

1. In a small bowl, whisk together the lime juice, scallion, tomatillo salsa, jalapeño, if using, and salt.

2. Add the avocado chunks and stir to combine.

3. Mash the avocado chunks with a fork to your preferred consistency. Serve with tortillas or chips.

BRATWURSTS in a BLANKET

The slight tartness and full porkiness of the Trader Joe's Bavarian sausages make them fabulously addictive.

2 tablespoons Dijon mustard

1 tablespoon honey

1 (8-ounce) can Trader Joe's Crescent Rolls

1 (7-ounce) package Trader Joe's Fully-Cooked Bavarian Bratwurst (8 sausages)

Yield: 8 bratwursts in a blanket
Prep Time: 10 minutes
Cook Time: 20 minutes

1. Preheat the oven to 375°F. Spray a baking sheet with cooking spray.

2. In a small bowl, combine the mustard and honey, stirring to thoroughly mix.

3. Unroll the crescent rolls from their can, placing them on a cutting board with the longest side of each crescent roll toward the bottom. Place a drop of the honey mustard on the bottom part of each crescent roll, followed by a bratwurst on top of the mustard. Set aside the remaining honey mustard.

4. Starting at the bottom of each roll, roll up the bratwurst in the crescent dough. Place the rolled bratwursts on the prepared baking sheet, making sure they are not touching each other.

5. Bake until the crescent rolls are golden brown, 18 to 20 minutes. Serve with the remaining honey mustard sauce.

THAI RED CURRY DEVILED EGGS

The secret ingredient in these babies is Trader Joe's Thai Red Curry Sauce, which adds an exotic flair.

1 (9.3-ounce) package Trader Joe's Cage Free Fresh Hard-Cooked Peeled Eggs (6 eggs)

2 tablespoons mayonnaise

2 tablespoons Trader Joe's Thai Red Curry Sauce

1 teaspoon lime juice

1 scallion, chopped, plus extra for garnish

¼ teaspoon kosher salt

Yield: 12 deviled eggs
Prep Time: 10 minutes
Cook Time: none

1. Cut each hard-cooked egg in half lengthwise. Scoop the yolks out into a small bowl.

2. Add the mayonnaise, curry sauce, lime juice, scallion, and salt to the bowl with the yolks. Mash the ingredients together until combined.

3. Spoon the yolk mixture into the egg white halves and garnish with a few pieces of scallion.

Note: If TJ's hard-cooked eggs are not available, see page 193.

JALAPEÑO CHEESE–STUFFED PEPPERS

Trader Joe's pub cheese is made from cheddar, and it's all-natural yet silky and spreadable.

1 (1-pint) package Trader Joe's Mini Sweet Bell Peppers

½ cup Trader Joe's Cheddar with Jalapeño Pub Cheese

5 to 6 slices Trader Joe's Fully Cooked Uncured Bacon

Yield: 24 stuffed pepper halves
Prep Time: 10 minutes
Cook Time: 10 minutes

1. Preheat the oven to 425°F. Spray a baking sheet with cooking spray.

2. Cut each mini pepper lengthwise and use a spoon to remove the seeds. Using a spoon, fill the pepper halves with pub cheese, place them on the prepared baking sheet, and bake until the cheese has melted, 5 to 8 minutes.

3. Meanwhile, arrange the bacon slices between layers of paper towels in a small microwave-safe dish. Microwave on high until crispy, 30 to 45 seconds. Crumble the bacon into bits.

4. Sprinkle the bacon over the cheesy peppers.

SPICY BONELESS CHICKEN PIECES

Coating Trader Joe's Mandarin Orange Chicken in a mixture of hot sauce and butter creates boneless buffalo wings in a snap.

¼ cup canola oil

1 (22-ounce) package Trader Joe's Mandarin Orange Chicken

½ cup Trader Joe's Jalapeño Pepper Hot Sauce

4 tablespoons unsalted butter

¼ cup honey

Yield: 4 servings
Prep Time: 10 minutes
Cook Time: 15 minutes

1. Line a plate with a paper towel. Heat the oil in a large skillet over medium-high heat until shimmering.

2. Discard the orange sauce from the chicken. Add the chicken pieces to the skillet and cook until crispy, 8 to 10 minutes, turning them over halfway through. Transfer the chicken to the prepared plate.

3. In a microwave-safe dish, place the hot sauce, butter, and honey. Microwave on high until the butter is melted and the sauce is warm, about 1 minute. Pour the hot sauce mixture into a large bowl along with the chicken pieces. Coat the chicken pieces with the hot sauce.

SLOPPY JOE NACHOS

This playful spin on nachos is Super Bowl food at its best.

1 (12-ounce) package frozen Trader Joe's Turkey Bolognese

1½ tablespoons brown sugar

1 tablespoon vinegar

1 tablespoon ketchup

½ (11.5-ounce) jar Trader Joe's Queso Cheese Dip

½ (16-ounce) bag Trader Joe's Organic Yellow Corn Tortilla Chip Rounds

Yield: 4 servings
Prep Time: 5 minutes
Cook Time: 10 minutes

1. Microwave the turkey Bolognese according to the package directions.

2. Carefully remove the Bolognese from the microwave. Add the brown sugar, vinegar, and ketchup to the carton, stirring to combine.

3. Pour the queso dip into a microwave-safe dish and microwave on high until warm, 2 to 3 minutes.

4. Layer a plate with the tortilla chips and pour the warm Bolognese mixture over the top. Drizzle the queso dip over the chips.

PINWHEELS with SPINACH and PROSCIUTTO

Italian for "ham," prosciutto is ham that has been seasoned, salt cured, air dried, and pressed.

1 tablespoon flour

1 (8-ounce) can Trader Joe's Crescent Rolls

1 (4-ounce) package Trader Joe's Sliced Prosciutto

½ cup Trader Joe's Sour Cream Spinach Dip

Yield: about 20 pinwheels
Prep Time: 10 minutes
Cook Time: 15 minutes

1. Preheat the oven to 400°F. Spray a baking sheet with cooking spray.

2. Dust a cutting board with the flour. Transfer the crescent dough in one piece from the tube onto the cutting board. Roll the dough out into a rectangle and pinch the creases together.

3. Layer the dough with 3 pieces of prosciutto, spread the spinach dip in an even layer on top of the prosciutto, then layer 3 more pieces of prosciutto on top.

4. Roll the dough up into a log, starting with the long side of the rectangle. Cut the log into rounds about ¾ inch thick. Arrange the pinwheels on the prepared baking sheet so they aren't touching each other.

5. Bake until the dough is golden brown, about 15 minutes.

FRITO PIE

Frito Pie is a Texan dish that pairs corn chips with chili and cheese. This is prime football-watching food.

½ (4-ounce) can Trader Joe's New Mexico Hatch Valley Fire Roasted Diced Green Chiles

½ cup sour cream

kosher salt

½ (14½-ounce) bag Trader Joe's Organic Corn Chip Dippers

½ (15-ounce) can Trader Joe's Beef Chili with Beans

1 cup Trader Joe's Shredded Cheddar Cheese

Yield: 4 servings
Prep Time: 10 minutes
Cook Time: 5 minutes

1. In a small bowl, combine the green chiles and sour cream. Add salt to taste and stir.

2. Microwave the chili on high until warm, 2 to 3 minutes.

3. On a large plate, spread the chips in a single layer. Pour the chili on top of the chips and sprinkle with the cheese. Garnish with dollops of the green chile sour cream.

PORK BUNS with BROCCOLI SLAW

Barbecued pork and coleslaw are a tasty combo that gets an Asian spin in this recipe.

1½ cups Trader Joe's Organic Cruciferous Slaw

⅓ cup mayonnaise

1 teaspoon Trader Joe's Jalapeño Pepper Hot Sauce (optional)

1 teaspoon soy sauce

2 teaspoons white vinegar

1 (8-ounce) package frozen Trader Ming's Chinese Style Pork Buns

Yield: 4 pork buns
Prep Time: 5 minutes
Cook Time: 5 minutes

1. Stir together the slaw, mayonnaise, hot sauce, if using, soy sauce, and vinegar in a medium bowl.

2. Place the pork buns on a microwave-safe dish and cover with a damp paper towel. Microwave on high until warm, about 45 seconds.

3. Carefully cut off the top one-third of each pork bun, discarding the extra dough. Pile the slaw onto the pork buns and serve open-faced.

CHEESY MOVIE NIGHT POPCORN

Nothing compares with the taste of popcorn made the old-fashioned way on the stovetop. But this recipe also works with 1 bag of microwaved popcorn if you want to skip to the second paragraph of the instructions.

2 tablespoons Trader Joe's Canola Oil

⅓ cup Trader Joe's Organic Popping Corn

2 tablespoons Trader Joe's Unsalted Butter, divided

1½ cups Trader Joe's Reduced Fat Cheese Puffs, divided

½ teaspoon kosher salt

Yield: 4 servings
Prep Time: 5 minutes
Cook Time: 8 minutes

1. Add the oil to a large heavy-duty pot. Add a few popcorn kernels and heat on medium-high.

When the kernels pop, immediately pour in all of the popping corn. Cover with a lid and reduce the heat to medium. Shake the pot occasionally. Remove the pot from the heat only when the popping slows down to a few seconds between each pop.

2. Meanwhile, to a heatproof bowl, add the butter. Microwave for 30 seconds to 1 minute until the butter is fully melted. Add the cheese puffs to a large resealable bag and seal. Pound on the bag with your hands or a rolling pin to crush the cheese puffs into a cheese dust.

3. To a large bowl or brown paper bag, add all of the popcorn. Drizzle with the salt, some of the butter, and some of the cheese dust. Toss to combine. Repeat with the remaining butter and cheese dust, tossing to combine again. Serve immediately.

MINI TOSTADAS with BEEF BRISKET

Tortilla chips are layered with brisket and melted pimento cheese for heavenly mini tostadas.

1 (16-ounce) package Trader Joe's Pulled Beef Brisket in Smoky BBQ Sauce

½ (16-ounce) bag Trader Joe's Organic Blue Corn Tortilla Chips

1 cup Trader Joe's Pimento Cheese Dip

Yield: 4 servings
Prep Time: 10 minutes
Cook Time: 5 minutes

1. Preheat the oven to 400°F. Line a rimmed baking sheet with foil.

2. Microwave the beef brisket according to the package directions.

3. On the prepared baking sheet, spread a layer of tortilla chips. Using a fork, add a little beef brisket to each chip, followed by a layer of pimento cheese.

4. Bake until the cheese has melted, about 5 minutes.

SWEET CHILI WINGS

Trader Joe's has many sauces to inspire your wings, and I enjoy the sweet and spicy flavor of the Sweet Chili Sauce.

12 Trader Joe's Organic Free Range Split Chicken Wings

1 teaspoon baking soda

1 teaspoon kosher salt

¾ cup Trader Joe's Sweet Chili Sauce

¼ cup cold unsalted butter, cut into pieces

1 tablespoon Trader Joe's Jalapeño Pepper Hot Sauce (optional)

Yield: 12 wings
Prep Time: 5 minutes
Cook Time: 30 minutes

1. Preheat the oven to 425°F. Line a rimmed baking sheet with foil.

2. Place the wings on the prepared baking sheet, sprinkle with the baking soda and salt, and toss to coat the wings. Spread the wings in a single layer and bake until crispy and the meat is fully cooked, 20 to 25 minutes.

3. Combine the chili sauce, butter, and hot sauce, if using, in a microwave-safe dish. Microwave on high until the butter is melted and the sauce is warm, about 1 minute. Stir.

4. Transfer the wings to a large bowl and add the sauce. Using a large spoon or tongs, toss the cooked wings with the sauce to coat.

Note: The baking soda makes for a crispier hot wing.

CHAPTER 3

SANDWICHES & SALADS

Sandwiches and salads are the go-to lunch option for many people, but it's easy to get stuck in a rut. Before you know it, you're eating the same ham and cheese every day of the week. That's an avoidable problem—think of sandwiches and salads as empty canvases on which you can put just about any meat, cheese, vegetable, and sauce. And the options for salads are just as vast. Trader Joe's makes it easy with options like pulled pork that's been smoked for hours or eggs that are already hard-cooked. Your only job is to put it all together.

And don't feel like you can make only these recipes to pack for lunch. Egg Salad Sandwiches or BLT are perfect to munch on while trekking to class in the morning, and a Muffuletta Sandwich or Barbecue Salad with Ranch Dressing is hearty enough to satisfy dinnertime hunger.

TRADITIONAL GRILLED CHEESE SANDWICHES

Shredded cheese makes for easier melting, and the thick brioche is the bread of choice—but any bread will do in a pinch.

4 slices Trader Joe's Sliced French Brioche

Trader Joe's Dijon Mustard, as needed

1 cup Trader Joe's Shredded Pepper Jack Cheese Blend

2 tablespoons unsalted butter, divided

Yield: 2 sandwiches
Prep Time: 5 minutes
Cook Time: 5 minutes

1. Spread 2 slices of the bread with the mustard. Mound each slice of bread with the shredded cheese and top with another slice of bread.

2. In a large nonstick pan, melt 1 tablespoon of butter over medium-high heat. Add both sandwiches to the pan and flatten them with a spatula.

3. Cook until the bottom sides are golden, 1 to 2 minutes.

4. Add the remaining 1 tablespoon of butter to the pan, and flip the sandwiches over. Cook until the second side is golden, 1 to 2 minutes.

PIZZA GRILLED CHEESE SANDWICHES

Mayonnaise is the not-so-secret ingredient that gets each grilled cheese sandwich golden and crispy in a pizza variation everyone will love.

2 tablespoons mayonnaise

4 slices Trader Joe's Sourdough Bread

1 cup Trader Joe's Shredded Pizza Seasoned Toscano Cheese, divided

8 pepperoni slices

1 medium tomato, thinly sliced, or 2 tablespoons Trader Joe's Julienne Sliced Sun Dried Tomatoes in Olive Oil

Yield: 2 sandwiches
Prep Time: 5 minutes
Cook Time: 6 minutes

1. Spread the mayonnaise onto 1 side of each bread slice. On a cutting board, arrange 2 slices of bread, mayonnaise-side down.

2. Divide ½ cup of cheese between the 2 bread slices. Top with the pepperoni and tomatoes. Then top with the remaining ½ cup of cheese. Top with the remaining 2 bread slices, mayonnaise-side up.

3. Heat a large nonstick pan on medium heat. Add the sandwiches to the pan and cook for 2 to 3 minutes per side, until golden.

GRILLED CHICKEN STRIPS on NAAN with RED PEPPER SPREAD

Trader Joe's Red Pepper Spread with Eggplant and Garlic adds a massive spark of flavor to enhance this sandwich.

2 pieces Trader Joe's Masala Tandoori Naan

2 tablespoons Trader Joe's Red Pepper Spread with Eggplant and Garlic

½ (12-ounce) package Trader Joe's Grilled Chicken Strips

4 slices Swiss cheese

Yield: 2 sandwiches
Prep Time: 10 minutes
Cook Time: 1 minute

1. Arrange the naan in a microwave-safe dish. Spread 1 tablespoon of red pepper spread on top of each piece of naan. Layer with the chicken strips and top with the cheese.

2. Microwave on high until the cheese is melted, about 1 minute.

MUFFULETTA SANDWICHES

A New Orleans specialty, the muffuletta sandwich is a crusty roll filled with meat like ham and salami and topped with a mixture of chopped olives.

2 Trader Joe's Ciabatta Rolls or Everything Ciabatta rolls

yellow mustard, as needed

1½ tablespoons Trader Joe's Green Olive Tapenade

4 slices turkey bologna

½ (7-ounce) package Trader Joe's Smoked Turkey Breast

2 slices Swiss cheese

2 Roma tomatoes, sliced

Yield: 2 sandwiches
Prep Time: 10 minutes
Cook Time: none

1. Slice each ciabatta in half. Spread the bottom layer of each ciabatta with mustard and the top with tapenade. On the bottom half of each sandwich, layer the bologna, turkey, cheese, and tomato.

2. Cover with the top layers and cut each sandwich in half.

TUNA SALAD SANDWICHES

It's the addition of a little lemon juice along with the sweetness of the relish that make this tuna salad recipe shine.

3½ tablespoons mayonnaise, divided

1 teaspoon lemon juice

½ teaspoon salt

¼ teaspoon ground pepper

2 tablespoons Trader Joe's Organic Sweet Pickle Relish

2 (5-ounce) cans Trader Joe's Albacore Solid White Tuna in Water, drained

4 slices Trader Joe's Texas Toast, or any other sandwich bread

Yield: 2 sandwiches
Prep Time: 5 minutes
Cook Time: none

1. In a small bowl, combine 2½ tablespoons of mayonnaise and the lemon juice, salt, pepper, and relish, and stir to combine.

2. Mix in the tuna with a fork until combined. Taste and adjust the seasoning as needed.

3. Spread the remaining 1 tablespoon of mayonnaise among all 4 slices of bread.

4. Divide the tuna salad between 2 slices of bread, then top the salad with the remaining slices.

FRIED FISH SANDWICHES

Trader Joe's Panko Breaded Tilapia Fillet is fried fish at its best without all of the labor-intensive work.

1 fillet frozen Trader Joe's Panko Breaded Tilapia Fillets

2 tablespoons mayonnaise

2 teaspoons Trader Joe's Organic Sweet Pickle Relish

1 teaspoon lemon juice

2 Trader Joe's Honey Wheat Hamburger Buns

Yield: 2 sandwiches
Prep Time: 10 minutes
Cook Time: 25 minutes

1. Preheat the oven to 425°F. Line a rimmed baking sheet with foil.

2. Place the fish fillet on the prepared baking sheet and bake until hot, 20 to 25 minutes. Meanwhile, in a small bowl, make a tartar sauce by stirring together the mayonnaise, relish, and lemon juice.

3. Carefully remove the fish from the oven and split the fillet in half horizontally with a knife. Layer the bottom halves of the buns with the tartar sauce and fish. Add the bun tops.

The I ♥ TRADER JOE'S® COLLEGE COOKBOOK

BUFFALO CHICKEN WRAPS

Between the vinegary hot sauce, the crunchy carrots, and the creamy dip, this Buffalo Chicken Wrap has the best parts of spicy wings without all the mess.

2 Trader Joe's Handmade Flour Tortillas

2 tablespoons Trader Joe's Buffalo Style Chicken Dip

1 teaspoon Trader Joe's Jalapeño Pepper Hot Sauce

½ (6-ounce) package Trader Joe's Organic Oven Roasted Chicken Breast

½ cup shredded carrots

chopped lettuce, as needed

Trader Joe's Chunky Blue Cheese Dressing, to serve (optional)

Yield: 2 sandwiches
Prep Time: 5 minutes
Cook Time: none

1. Lay the tortillas on a cutting board. Spread the chicken dip in a line down the middle of each tortilla. Top with the hot sauce.

2. Onto each tortilla, layer the chicken, carrots, and lettuce on top of the dip. Roll the wraps burrito-style, tucking the bottom up before rolling sideways.

3. Dip in the blue cheese dressing, if using, while eating.

PULLED PORK SANDWICHES

Trader Joe's smoked pulled pork lets you enjoy all the delicious smokiness of the meat without the effort of having to make it yourself.

½ (16-ounce) package Pulled Pork in Sweet & Smokey BBQ Sauce

½ (10-ounce) bag shredded green cabbage

1 tablespoon mayonnaise

2 tablespoons chopped Trader Joe's Organic Sweet Bread and Butter Pickles, plus 1½ tablespoons pickle juice

kosher salt and freshly ground black pepper

4 Trader Joe's Michette Rolls, or other rolls

Yield: 4 sandwiches
Prep Time: 10 minutes
Cook Time: 5 minutes

1. Microwave the pulled pork according to the package directions.

2. In a small bowl, make the coleslaw by stirring together the cabbage, mayonnaise, chopped pickles, and pickle juice. Season to taste with salt and pepper.

3. Spread pulled pork on the bottom half of each roll. Add the coleslaw and the top halves of the rolls.

EGG SALAD SANDWICHES

Celery adds a slight crunch to contrast with the silkiness of the egg salad. For extra oomph, add ham or even prosciutto.

1 (9.3-ounce) package Trader Joe's Cage Free Fresh Hard-Cooked Peeled Eggs (6 eggs)

3 tablespoons mayonnaise, divided

¼ teaspoon salt

¼ teaspoon freshly ground black pepper

1 celery rib, chopped

4 slices Trader Joe's Soft 10 Grain Bread, or another type of bread, toasted if desired

Yield: 2 sandwiches
Prep Time: 5 minutes
Cook Time: 5 minutes

1. In a small bowl, mash the hard-cooked eggs with a fork. Add 2 tablespoons of mayonnaise and the salt, pepper, and celery, and stir to combine. Taste and adjust the seasonings as needed.

2. Spread the bread slices with the remaining 1 tablespoon of mayonnaise. Mound the egg salad onto 2 slices of bread, then top with the remaining slices.

Note: If TJ's hard-cooked eggs are not available, see page 193.

BLT SANDWICHES

Does it get any better than a sandwich stuffed with crisp bacon, tomatoes, and crunchy lettuce?

8 slices Trader Joe's Fully Cooked Uncured Bacon

½ cup Trader Joe's Julienne Sliced Sun Dried Tomatoes in Olive Oil, drained

¼ cup mayonnaise

kosher salt and freshly ground black pepper

4 slices Trader Joe's Soft 10 Grain Bread, toasted

¼ cup lettuce leaves

Yield: 2 sandwiches
Prep Time: 5 minutes
Cook Time: 1 minute

1. Arrange the bacon slices between layers of paper towels in a microwave-safe dish. Microwave on high power until crispy, 30 seconds to 1 minute.

2. In a small bowl, stir together the sun dried tomatoes and mayonnaise to combine. Season to taste with salt and pepper, and stir again.

3. Spread tomato mayonnaise onto 2 bread slices. Layer with bacon slices and lettuce leaves. Top with the remaining 2 slices of bread.

CHILEAN-STYLE HOT DOGS

A friend from South America introduced me to Chilean-style hot dogs—hot dogs layered on hard buns with mayonnaise and slices of tomato and avocado.

4 Trader Joe's Honey Wheat Hot Dog Buns

4 Trader Joe's All Natural Uncured All-Beef Hot Dogs

mayonnaise, as needed

2 Roma tomatoes, sliced

1 avocado, sliced (for slicing tips, see page 192)

Yield: 4 hot dogs
Prep Time: 5 minutes
Cook Time: 3 minutes

1. Preheat the oven to 400°F. Arrange the hot dog buns on a baking sheet and place in the oven until toasted, just 1 to 2 minutes.

2. Meanwhile, wrap the hot dogs in a damp paper towel and microwave on high until hot, about 1 minute.

3. Carefully remove the toasted buns from the oven. Spread each bun with mayonnaise and add the hot dogs. Garnish each one with tomato and avocado slices.

MEATBALL SUBS

Trader Joe's Garlic & Cheese Bread Sticks are a great start to building a meatball sub.

½ (16-ounce) package frozen Trader Joe's Party Size Mini Meatballs, thawed

1 cup Trader Giotto's Organic Tomato Basil Marinara

½ (12-ounce) package Trader Joe's Garlic & Cheese Bread Sticks

½ cup Trader Joe's Shredded Pizza Seasoned Toscano Cheese

Yield: 4 subs
Prep Time: 10 minutes
Cook Time: 12 minutes

1. Preheat the oven to 400°F. Line a rimmed baking sheet with foil.

2. Cut each meatball in half and place in a microwave-safe dish. Microwave on high until slightly warm, about 1 minute. Pour the marinara sauce over the meatballs, and microwave on high until the sauce is warm, about 1 minute.

3. Using a serrated knife, split 4 bread sticks in half lengthwise, cutting only three quarters of the way through to keep the halves attached. Place the bread sticks on the prepared baking sheet, split-side up. Evenly divide the heated meatballs and marinara sauce between the split bread sticks. Top with the cheese.

4. Bake the sandwiches until the cheese is melted and the bread is toasted, 7 to 10 minutes.

TROPICAL FRUIT SALAD

Trader Joe's Organic Tropical Fruit Medley, which includes mango, pineapple, and papaya, serves as a starting point for the makings of a tasty fruit salad.

1 (16-ounce) container Trader Joe's Organic Tropical Fruit Medley

2 teaspoons honey

juice of ½ lemon

1 apple, cut into bite-size pieces

1 pear, cut into bite-size pieces

Yield: 2 servings
Prep Time: 10 minutes
Cook Time: none

1. Drain the tropical fruit, reserving the juices, and cut the fruit into bite-size pieces.

2. In a medium bowl, stir together the fruit juice, honey, and lemon juice. Add the chopped tropical fruit, apple, and pear, and stir.

CAESAR SALAD 2.0

By taking Trader Joe's Caesar salad and elevating it with a few Mediterranean ingredients, this dish has the makings of a meal.

1 (15-ounce) bag Trader Joe's Caesar Style with Croutons, Shredded Parmesan Cheese and Dressing

½ cup Trader Joe's Julienne Sliced Sun Dried Tomatoes in Olive Oil, drained

½ cup pitted kalamata olives

1 (12-ounce) package Trader Joe's Chicken Strips

Yield: 2 servings
Prep Time: 5 minutes
Cook Time: none

1. In a medium bowl, place the lettuce from the salad mix. Top the lettuce with the sun dried tomatoes, olives, and chicken. Toss to combine.

2. Add the cheese from the salad mix and drizzle with the dressing. Toss gently to combine.

BARBECUE SALAD with RANCH DRESSING

A blend of iceberg lettuce, romaine lettuce, and cabbage is perfect for a barbecue salad.

½ (16-ounce) bag Trader Joe's Pulled Pork in Sweet & Smokey BBQ Sauce or Trader Joe's Pulled Beef Brisket in Smoky BBQ Sauce

½ (16-ounce) bag any salad greens

2 Roma tomatoes, diced

1 cucumber, diced

½ cup Trader Joe's Fancy Shredded Mexican Cheese Blend

Trader Joe's Lowfat Parmesan Ranch Dressing, as needed

Yield: 2 servings
Prep Time: 10 minutes
Cook Time: 5 minutes

1. Microwave the pulled pork or beef according to the package directions.

2. In a medium bowl, place the salad, tomatoes, cucumber, and cheese. Drizzle with the ranch dressing and toss to combine.

3. Transfer the salad to plates and top with the pulled pork or beef.

CHICKEN SALAD–STUFFED TOMATOES

The apple adds a tartness to this sweet chicken salad and the celery brings a nice crunch, mandatory for any salad, in my book.

½ (12-ounce) container Trader Joe's Wine Country Chicken Salad with Cranberries and Pecans

½ Granny Smith apple, cut into bite-size pieces

½ cup chopped celery

kosher salt and freshly ground black pepper

4 Roma tomatoes

Yield: 2 servings
Prep Time: 10 minutes
Cook Time: none

1. In a small bowl, stir together the chicken salad, apple, and celery. Season to taste with salt and pepper.

2. Cut the top ¼ inch off each tomato. Hollow out each tomato and fill with chicken salad.

ANTIPASTO SALAD

The word antipasto *refers to the traditional first course of an Italian meal, which includes a platter of cured meats, artichokes, olives, and cheeses.*

½ (8-ounce) package sopressata salami

1 (14-ounce) can artichoke hearts, drained

1 (15.5-ounce) can Trader Joe's Cannellini White Kidney Beans, drained and rinsed

kosher salt and freshly ground black pepper

Yield: 2 servings
Prep Time: 10 minutes
Cook Time: none

1. Cube the salami into bite-size pieces. Place in a medium bowl.

2. Cut the artichokes in half and add to the bowl with the salami. Add the entire jar of beans to the bowl, stirring to combine. Season to taste with salt and pepper.

GREEK PASTA SALAD

This pasta salad can be eaten warm, cold, or at room temperature. It's easy to whip up and will please a crowd without costing a ton of cash.

½ teaspoon kosher salt, plus more for boiling the pasta

2 (10-ounce) packages Trader Joe's Perline Pasta and Prosciutto

juice of 1 lemon

⅓ cup olive oil

½ teaspoon dried oregano or dried thyme (optional)

¼ teaspoon freshly ground black pepper

1 pint grape tomatoes

1 cucumber, peeled and chopped into bite-size pieces

1½ cups Trader Joe's Marinated Artichokes, cut into bite-size pieces

⅓ cup Trader Joe's Feta Cheese with Mediterranean Herbs

Yield: 4 servings
Prep Time: 10 minutes
Cook Time: 3 minutes

1. Bring a medium pot of salted water to a boil over high heat. Cook the perline pasta until al dente (see page 193), 2 to 3 minutes. Drain the pasta in a colander.

2. Meanwhile, in a large bowl, whisk together the lemon juice, olive oil, oregano, salt, and pepper.

3. Add the pasta to the bowl with the dressing, along with the tomatoes, cucumber, and artichoke hearts. Stir with a large spoon. Taste and adjust the seasonings with salt and pepper, as needed. Top with the cheese.

CHAPTER 4

SOUPS

To break it down plain and simple, soup just makes me happy. In my world, there's nothing more comforting than slurping a bowl of homemade soup. Most complaints about making soup are about it being too time-consuming. Not so with these recipes, thanks to Trader Joe's easy ingredients. And words cannot even describe my love for Trader Joe's Savory Chicken Flavor. It takes up so little room in the cabinet compared to its equivalent of chicken broth cans. As long as you're stocked with these little packets, homemade soup in minutes is within reach.

It's worth noting that for an avid soup maker, an immersion blender is an inexpensive, worthwhile investment: it's compact and allows you to purée soups right in the pot.

MISO SOUP with TOFU and SPINACH

Adding spinach and tofu to Trader Joe's Instant Miso Soup really bulks it up into a heartier vegan meal.

3 cups water

2 (.94-ounce) packets Trader Joe's Instant Miso Soup

½ (6-ounce) bag baby spinach

½ (14-ounce) package Trader Joe San Firm Organic Tofu, cut into bite-size pieces

2 scallions, chopped, for garnish (optional)

Yield: 2 servings
Prep Time: 5 minutes
Cook Time: 10 minutes

1. In a small pot, bring the water to a boil over high heat. Whisk in the soup mix. Add the spinach, stirring until wilted, about 1 minute, then add the tofu pieces and stir.

2. Remove the soup from heat and ladle it into bowls. Garnish with the scallions, if using.

THAI CARROT SOUP

This dairy-free soup is a blend of flavors that tastes like it takes much longer to prepare than it does.

1 (10-ounce) bag shredded carrots

1 (14-ounce) can light coconut milk

1 cup vegetable broth

½ cup Trader Joe's Thai Yellow Curry Sauce

kosher salt and freshly ground black pepper

Yield: 2 servings
Prep Time: 5 minutes
Cook Time: 25 minutes

1. Coarsely chop the shredded carrots into bite-size pieces.

2. Add the carrots, coconut milk, vegetable broth, and curry sauce to a medium pot and bring to a boil over high heat. Once the soup is boiling, reduce the heat to medium and simmer until the carrots are fully cooked, 15 to 20 minutes.

3. Season to taste with salt and pepper.

CURRIED LENTIL SOUP

Lentils can take a little time to cook, but not so with the already prepared beluga lentils from Trader Joe's.

½ tablespoon canola oil

½ (14.5-ounce) container Trader Joe's Mirepoix

2 cups vegetable broth

½ (17.6-ounce) package Trader Joe's Steamed Lentils

¼ cup Trader Joe's Thai Red Curry Sauce

1 tablespoon curry powder

juice of ½ lemon

kosher salt and freshly ground black pepper

Yield: 2 servings
Prep Time: 5 minutes
Cook Time: 15 minutes

1. In a medium pot, heat the oil over medium heat until shimmering. Add the mirepoix and sauté until the vegetables are slightly softened, about 5 minutes.

2. Add the vegetable broth, lentils, curry sauce, curry powder, and lemon juice, stirring to combine. Let the soup simmer over medium heat for about 10 minutes.

3. Season to taste with salt and pepper.

Note: Mirepoix is a mixture of chopped carrots, celery, and onions that's a base for many soup, stew, and sauce recipes. Trader Joe's makes it easy by doing all the chopping for you.

BLACK BEAN SOUP with CHIMICHURRI RICE

It's the comfort of rice and beans transformed into vegetarian soup. Eat this soup immediately after preparing it—otherwise, the rice soaks up the liquid.

1 (32-ounce) container Trader Joe's Latin Style Black Bean Soup

1 (16-ounce) package frozen Trader Joe's Peruvian Style Chimichurri Rice, thawed

shredded cheddar cheese, sour cream, and scallions, for garnish (optional)

Yield: 4 servings
Prep Time: 5 minutes
Cook Time: 10 minutes

1. To a medium pot, add the soup and bring it to a boil over high heat.

2. To the pot, stir in the rice. Reduce the heat to medium and simmer for 5 minutes to let the rice warm. Serve immediately, garnished with cheese, sour cream, and scallions, if using.

DOUBLE BUTTERNUT SQUASH SOUP with ITALIAN SAUSAGE RAVIOLI

With both a butternut squash soup base and squash, this soup's sweetness is balanced nicely with the salty bite from the Italian sausage and cheese ravioli.

1 (12-ounce) bag Trader Joe's Cut Butternut Squash

½ (32-ounce) box Trader Joe's Organic Low Sodium Butternut Squash Soup

½ cup water

½ teaspoon kosher salt

½ teaspoon freshly ground black pepper

1 (9-ounce) package Trader Joe's Italian Sausage & 4-Cheese Ravioli

Yield: 2 servings
Prep Time: 8 minutes
Cook Time: 15 minutes

1. Microwave the butternut squash according to the package directions. Carefully transfer it from the plastic package to a cutting board. Let cool for a couple of minutes, then chop the squash into bite-size pieces.

2. Add the butternut squash soup, water, salt, and pepper to a medium pot and bring to a boil over high heat. Add the ravioli, making sure that all the ravioli pieces are submerged in the liquid. Reduce the heat to medium and cook until the ravioli is tender, 8 to 10 minutes.

3. Remove the soup from the heat and stir in the squash pieces. Serve immediately.

MEXICAN TORTILLA SOUP with AVOCADO and TORTILLA CHIPS

The chicken and tomato base is enhanced by the richness of avocado, the crunch of tortilla chips, and the flavors of Mexican seasonings.

2 cups chicken broth, or 2 cups hot water plus 2 (9.6-gram) pouches Trader Joe's Savory Chicken Flavor

½ (28-ounce) can Trader Joe's Diced Organic Tomatoes in Tomato Juice

2 tablespoons Trader Joe's Taco Seasoning Mix, or more to taste

½ teaspoon kosher salt, or more taste

¼ teaspoon freshly ground black pepper, or more to taste

1 (12-ounce) package Trader Joe's Just Chicken White Meat, chopped into smaller pieces

juice of 1 lime

1 ounce cilantro, leaves plucked from stems

1 avocado, diced (for dicing tips, see page 192)

¼ (16-ounce) bag Trader Joe's Salsa Tortilla Chips, crumbled

Yield: 2 servings
Prep Time: 15 minutes
Cook Time: 20 minutes

1. In a medium pot, add the chicken broth, tomatoes, taco seasoning, salt, and pepper, and stir to combine. Bring to a boil over high heat. Reduce the heat to medium-low. Add the chicken pieces and lime juice and simmer for 10 minutes.

2. Adjust the seasoning with salt, pepper, or taco seasoning, as needed. Garnish with cilantro, avocado, and crumbled chips.

CHICKEN and DUMPLINGS

Chicken and dumplings usually takes a lot of work. The shortcut here is the buttermilk biscuits, which simmer in the chicken broth to create airy, fluffy dumplings.

4 cups chicken broth, or 4 cups hot water plus 4 (9.6-gram) pouches Trader Joe's Savory Chicken Flavor

½ (16-ounce) can Trader Joe's Buttermilk Biscuits (4 biscuits)

1 (16-ounce) package Trader Joe's Just Chicken White Meat

½ teaspoon kosher salt

¼ teaspoon freshly ground black pepper

2 tablespoons chopped chives (optional)

Yield: 2 servings
Prep Time: 10 minutes
Cook Time: 20 minutes

1. In a medium pot, bring the chicken broth to a boil over high heat.

2. Meanwhile, remove the 4 biscuits from the package and cut each biscuit into three rows horizontally and vertically, creating 9 pieces from each biscuit.

3. When the chicken broth begins boiling, carefully drop in each biscuit piece.

4. Reduce the heat to medium and cover the pot. Cook until the biscuit pieces are fully cooked and soft, about 15 minutes. Use a slotted spoon to remove 1 dumpling; cut it in half and taste to check for doneness.

5. Stir in the chicken pieces, salt, and pepper. Cook until the chicken is hot throughout, 2 to 3 minutes, and garnish with chives, if using.

Note: The biscuits must be dropped into the liquid individually or they'll stick together.

ANDOUILLE and CHICKPEA SOUP

The Trader Joe's Cumin and Chili Chickpeas are infused with so much garlic and spice goodness that they add a bolt of flavor to the soup.

½ (12.8-ounce) package Trader Joe's Smoked Andouille Chicken Sausage (2 sausages)

1 teaspoon canola oil

2 cups chicken broth, or 2 cups hot water plus 2 (9.6-gram) pouches Trader Joe's Savory Chicken Flavor

½ (15-ounce) can chickpeas, drained

1 (8-ounce) package Trader Joe's Cumin and Chili Chickpeas

1 tablespoon minced ginger

½ teaspoon kosher salt

½ teaspoon freshly ground black pepper

1 (6-ounce) bag baby spinach

Yield: 2 servings
Prep Time: 10 minutes
Cook Time: 25 minutes

1. Slice the sausages lengthwise and then cut each half into bite-size pieces.

2. In a large saucepan, heat the oil over medium-high heat until shimmering. Add the sausage and sauté until golden, 6 to 8 minutes, stirring occasionally. Remove the sausage from the pan and set aside.

3. In a medium pot, add the chicken broth, canned chickpeas, packaged chickpeas, ginger, salt, and pepper, and bring to a simmer over medium-high heat. Simmer for 5 to 8 minutes. Add the spinach and stir until it wilts, just a couple of minutes. Add the reserved sausage pieces and stir to combine.

EGG DROP SOUP with CILANTRO-CHICKEN WONTONS

Egg drop soup is one of those delightfully simple recipes that's so easy—once you know how to make it, you'll be preparing it all the time.

3 cups chicken broth, or 3 cups hot water plus 3 (9.6-gram) pouches Trader Joe's Savory Chicken Flavor

1 (16-ounce) bag frozen Trader Ming's Asian Vegetables with Beijing Style Soy Sauce

1 (12-ounce) bag frozen Trader Joe's Chicken Cilantro Mini Wontons

2 large eggs

kosher salt and freshly ground black pepper

Yield: 2 servings
Prep Time: 5 minutes
Cook Time: 15 minutes

1. In a medium pot, bring the chicken broth to a boil over high heat.

2. Meanwhile, remove the soy sauce packet from the frozen vegetables and defrost it in the microwave until thawed, 1 to 2 minutes. Add the soy sauce packet to the chicken broth, stirring to combine. Once the broth is boiling, add the frozen vegetables. Reduce the heat to medium, and let the vegetables cook for 5 minutes. Add the mini wontons and cook for 2 to 3 minutes longer.

3. Meanwhile, crack the eggs into a small liquid measuring cup. Whisk the eggs with a fork until beaten.

4. Return the heat to high. When the broth is at a substantial boil, pour the beaten eggs in a thin, steady stream into the soup and stir the soup as the eggs hit the broth. Stir to combine. Season to taste with salt and pepper.

TURKEY and VEGETABLE CHILI

By using Trader Joe's Fully Cooked Turkey Bolognese and Trader Joe's Ratatouille, most of the work has already been done for you in this stew.

1 (12-ounce) package frozen Trader Joe's Turkey Bolognese

½ (1.3-ounce) packet Trader Joe's Taco Seasoning Mix

1 (25.75-ounce) jar Trader Joe's Garden Vegetable Soup

1 (15.5-ounce) can pinto beans

¼ teaspoon kosher salt

¼ teaspoon freshly ground black pepper

Trader Joe's Salsa Tortilla Chips, as needed

OPTIONAL TOPPINGS:
sour cream, grated cheese, salsa, pumpkin seeds

Yield: 4 servings
Prep Time: 5 minutes
Cook Time: 15 minutes

1. In a medium pot, add the turkey Bolognese and taco seasoning and stir to combine. Add the vegetable soup, pinto beans (liquid included), salt, and pepper. Bring to a boil over high heat. Then reduce the heat to low and let simmer for 10 minutes.

2. Ladle the chili into bowls and crumble tortilla chips on top. Serve with optional toppings, if using.

LOADED POTATO SOUP

Similar to a loaded baked potato with all the fixings, except in a dreamy soup.

½ (28-ounce) package frozen Trader Joe's Mashed Potatoes (about 25 medallions)

1 cup whole milk

2 cups chicken broth, or 2 cups hot water plus 2 (9.6-gram) pouches Trader Joe's Savory Chicken Flavor

½ teaspoon kosher salt

¼ teaspoon freshly ground black pepper

8 slices Trader Joe's Fully Cooked Uncured Bacon

2 scallions, chopped

½ (8-ounce) package Trader Joe's Shredded Pepper Jack Cheese Blend

Yield: 2 servings
Prep Time: 10 minutes
Cook Time: 15 to 20 minutes

1. In a medium pot, add the potatoes, milk, chicken broth, salt, and pepper, and heat over medium-high heat, stirring every few minutes, until the potatoes have melted, 10 to 15 minutes.

2. Meanwhile, arrange the bacon slices between layers of paper towels in a small microwave-safe dish. Microwave on high until crispy, 30 to 45 seconds. Crumble the bacon into bits and combine with the scallions and cheese in a small bowl.

3. Once the potato soup is thick and bubbling, ladle into bowls. Generously top with the bacon and cheese mixture.

TOMATO-MEATBALL SOUP with CHEESE

Grilled cheese and tomato soup—this is the best of both worlds in one bowl.

1 (15-ounce) can Trader Joe's Organic Tomato Sauce

1 cup water

1 cup half-and-half

½ teaspoon kosher salt

¼ teaspoon freshly ground black pepper

½ (20-ounce) package Trader Joe's Party Size Mini Meatballs

½ loaf Trader Joe's Ciabatta

4 slices Swiss cheese

Yield: 2 servings
Prep Time: 5 minutes
Cook Time: 15 minutes

1. Preheat the oven's broiler.

2. In a medium pot, combine the tomato sauce, water, half-and-half, salt, and pepper, and bring to a boil over high heat. Reduce the heat to medium and simmer. Add the meatballs and cook until hot, 5 to 8 minutes.

3. Meanwhile, slice the bread lengthwise. Place the bread on a rimmed baking sheet and layer each half with 2 slices of cheese. Put the bread under the broiler to toast, 2 to 3 minutes, checking it about every 30 seconds.

4. Cut the bread into bite-size crouton pieces. Ladle the soup into bowls and top with the cheese croutons.

Substitution: Milk can replace the half-and-half.

GAZPACHO

In warmer months when you crave soup but may not be too keen on eating hot food, try gazpacho, an uncooked soup hailing from Spain.

½ (28-ounce) can Trader Joe's Whole Peeled and Salted Plum Tomatoes with Basil

1 (12-ounce) container Trader Joe's Tzatziki

juice of ½ lemon, or more to taste

½ teaspoon kosher salt, or more to taste

Yield: 2 servings
Prep Time: 5 minutes
Cook Time: none

1. In a blender, add the tomatoes, tzatziki, lemon juice, and salt, and blend on high speed until combined, 30 seconds to 1 minute. If you don't have a blender, place the tomatoes in a large bowl and use your hands to break them into pieces, then add the other ingredients.

2. Taste and adjust the seasoning with salt and lemon juice, as needed.

3. Serve at room temperature, or let the gazpacho chill in the fridge for 1 to 2 hours prior to serving.

CHAPTER 5

PASTAS

P astas are among the easiest ways to quickly create a tasty dish. To this day when I'm short on time, I'll toss a batch of angel-hair pasta with butter and Parmesan cheese for a quick lunch or dinner that's easy, cheap, and—most essentially—tasty.

Of course, the first thing that pops into most people's heads when they think of pasta is a basic Italian red sauce, which you'll find in classic recipes like Spaghetti and Meatballs (page 75). The Italians may have mastered the art of pasta, but these recipes pull inspiration from all over the globe, using pasta to explore a wide array of flavor profiles, including those with a spark of Middle Eastern ingredients, like Chickpea Penne (page 66).

OLIVE OIL SPAGHETTI with ARUGULA

In Italy, spaghetti aglio e olio *refers to spaghetti noodles tossed with olive oil, garlic, and crushed red pepper flakes. This is an easy twist, which replaces the garlic with a kick of arugula.*

¼ (16-ounce package) Trader Giotto's Organic Spaghetti

1 tablespoon olive oil

¾ (12-ounce) container Trader Joe's Marinated Fresh Mozzarella, plus 3 to 4 tablespoons marinating oil

½ (7-ounce) bag arugula

½ teaspoon kosher salt

¼ teaspoon freshly ground black pepper

½ teaspoon red chile pepper flakes

Yield: 1 serving
Prep Time: 5 minutes
Cook Time: 15 minutes

1. Cook the spaghetti according to the package directions. Drain in a colander and toss with the olive oil.

2. Add 1 tablespoon marinade oil from the mozzarella to the now-empty pot and heat over medium-high heat until shimmering. Add the arugula, stirring constantly, until it wilts, 2 to 3 minutes. Remove from the heat.

3. Add the pasta to the pot along with the salt, pepper, chile pepper flakes, mozzarella, and 2 to 3 tablespoons marinade oil. Toss to combine.

CHICKPEA PENNE

Easiest. Pasta. Ever. The Trader Joe's Channa Masala is a mix of tomatoes, chickpeas, and spices, which adds a Middle Eastern flair.

½ (16-ounce) package Trader Joe's Organic Penne Rigate

1 (10-ounce) package Trader Joe's Channa Masala

¼ teaspoon kosher salt

¼ teaspoon freshly ground black pepper

Yield: 2 servings
Prep Time: none
Cook Time: 15 minutes

1. Bring a medium pot of salted water to a boil on high heat. Cook the penne according to package directions.

2. Meanwhile, pierce a few holes in the plastic film on the channa masala. Microwave on high power until warm, 4 to 4½ minutes.

3. When the penne is done, drain it in a colander. Add the heated channa masala to the pot (off the heat), along with the cooked penne. Season with salt and pepper. Stir to combine and serve immediately.

EGGPLANT SPAGHETTI

Trader Joe's Eggplant Parmesan is transformed into delicious tomato pasta studded with breaded bits of eggplant.

½ (16-ounce) package Trader Giotto's Organic Spaghetti

1 tablespoon olive oil

1½ cups Trader Giotto's Roasted Garlic Spaghetti Sauce

1 (16-ounce) bag frozen Trader Giotto's Misto alla Griglia, thawed

½ teaspoon kosher salt

¼ teaspoon freshly ground black pepper

Yield: 2 servings
Prep Time: 5 minutes
Cook Time: 20 minutes

1. Cook the spaghetti according to the package directions. Drain and toss with the olive oil.

2. Heat the marinara sauce in a medium skillet over medium-high heat. Cut each eggplant piece into quarters. Add the contents of the eggplant to the skillet, along with the salt and pepper. Stir to combine and cook until hot, about 5 minutes.

3. Add the pasta to the pan and gently toss to combine.

EGGPLANT AND GARLIC CAPELLINI

The Bulgarian-style Trader Joe's Eggplant Garlic Spread is a tasty base for this Mediterranean-inspired pasta.

½ (16-ounce) package Trader Joe's Italian Capellini

1 tablespoon plus 1 teaspoon olive oil

2 medium tomatoes, diced

1 (12-ounce) jar Trader Joe's Eggplant Garlic Spread

juice of 1 lemon

½ teaspoon kosher salt

¼ teaspoon freshly ground black pepper

Yield: 2 servings
Prep Time: 5 minutes
Cook Time: 15 minutes

1. Cook the capellini according to the package directions. Reserve ⅓ cup of pasta water, then drain the pasta and toss with 1 tablespoon of olive oil.

2. In a medium skillet, warm the remaining 1 teaspoon of olive oil over medium-high heat until shimmering. Add the tomatoes and sauté just a few minutes, stirring constantly, until the tomatoes are cooked. Add the eggplant spread, lemon juice, reserved pasta water, salt, and pepper and stir to combine. Reduce the heat to medium-low and simmer for 5 minutes.

3. Add the pasta to the skillet and toss to coat with the sauce.

PORTABELLA MUSHROOM TRIANGOLI

These ravioli stuffed with mushrooms and provolone cheese have so much flavor that they need only a minimal coating in this light sauce.

2 (8.8-ounce) packages Trader Joe's Porcini Mushroom and Truffle Triangoli

1 tablespoon olive oil

2 teaspoons Trader Joe's Crushed Garlic

2 tablespoons Trader Joe's Coastal Sauvignon Blanc, or any other dry white wine

⅓ cup chicken broth

1 tablespoon unsalted butter

½ teaspoon kosher salt

¼ teaspoon freshly ground black pepper

Trader Joe's Grated Parmigiano-Reggiano cheese, as needed (optional)

Yield: 2 servings
Prep Time: 5 minutes
Cook Time: 10 minutes

1. Cook the ravioli according to the package directions. Drain.

2. In a medium skillet over high heat, heat the olive oil until shimmering. Add the garlic and cook for 15 to 30 seconds. Add the wine, chicken broth, butter, salt, and pepper to the pan, stirring and cooking until the butter melts.

3. Add the ravioli to the sauce, remove from the heat, and carefully toss to combine. Top with cheese, if using.

CAPELLINI with SMOKED SARDINES, GARLIC, and PINE NUTS

Capellini is one of my favorite pastas to use because of the amazingly quick cooking time.

½ (16-ounce) package Trader Joe's Italian Capellini

2 tablespoons olive oil, divided

1 (4.25-ounce) tin Trader Joe's Lightly Smoked Sardines in Olive Oil

½ teaspoon kosher salt

¼ teaspoon freshly ground black pepper

1 teaspoon Trader Joe's Crushed Garlic

2 tablespoons Trader Joe's Dry Roasted Pignolias (pine nuts, see page 194)

Yield: 2 servings
Prep Time: 5 minutes
Cook Time: 12 minutes

1. Cook the capellini according to the package directions. Drain and toss with 1 tablespoon of olive oil.

2. In a medium skillet, heat the sardines and 1 tablespoon of olive oil over medium-high heat. Use a spatula to break up the sardines and combine them with the oil. When the sardines have melded with the oil, add the salt, pepper, garlic, and pine nuts. Cook, stirring constantly, until the garlic and pine nuts are golden, 1 to 2 minutes.

3. Remove from the heat, add the pasta to the sauce, and toss well.

FARFALLE with VODKA SAUCE

Farfalle pasta resembles butterflies or bow ties, so it's often paired with chunkier sauces.

½ (16-ounce) package Trader Joe's Farfalle Pasta

1½ tablespoons olive oil, divided

2½ ounces basil, leaves plucked from stem

½ (25-ounce) Trader Giotto's Organic Vodka Sauce

1 cup Trader Giotto's Traditional Fresh Ricotta

Yield: 2 servings
Prep Time: 5 minutes
Cook Time: 15 minutes

1. Cook the farfalle according to the package directions. Drain and toss with 1 tablespoon of olive oil.

2. In the pot used for the pasta, warm the remaining ½ tablespoon of olive oil over medium-high heat until shimmering. Add the basil and stir until the basil is wilted, 30 seconds to 1 minute.

3. Add the vodka sauce to the pot and stir to combine. Let the sauce cook until hot, just a few minutes. Remove the pot from the heat. Stir in the ricotta and pasta.

SPAGHETTI PUTTANESCA

Puttanesca is an Italian tomato sauce with tomatoes, capers, olives, anchovies, and garlic. Here, delicate smoked sardines fill in for the harsher taste of anchovies.

½ (16-ounce) package Trader Giotto's Organic Spaghetti

1 tablespoon olive oil

1 (15-ounce) can Trader Joe's Organic Tomato Sauce

¼ (4.25-ounce) tin Trader Joe's Lightly Smoked Sardines in Olive Oil

2 teaspoons Trader Joe's Crushed Garlic

2 tablespoons Trader Joe's Olive Tapenade Spread

1 tablespoon capers, rinsed and chopped

Yield: 2 servings
Prep Time: 5 minutes
Cook Time: 15 minutes

1. Cook the spaghetti according to the package directions. Reserve ½ cup of pasta water, then drain the pasta and toss with the olive oil.

2. In a medium pot, add the tomato sauce, reserved pasta water, sardines, garlic, tapenade, and capers. Cook over medium heat, stirring frequently. Let simmer for 10 minutes.

3. Add the pasta and toss to combine.

SEAFOOD FETTUCCINI

Trader Joe's Frozen Seafood Blend—a mix of shrimp, calamari, and bay scallops—is an affordable way to get a wide array of seafood into your diet.

¼ (16-ounce) package Trader Joe's Organic Whole Wheat Fettuccini or Trader Joe's Authentic Fettuccine

2 tablespoons olive oil, divided

½ (16-ounce) package Trader Joe's Seafood Blend, thawed

½ cup white wine

2 tablespoons unsalted butter

Yield: 2 servings
Prep Time: 5 minutes
Cook Time: 15 minutes

1. Cook the fettuccini according to the package directions. Drain and toss with 1 tablespoon of olive oil.

2. In a medium skillet, heat the remaining 1 tablespoon of olive oil over medium-high heat until shimmering. Add the defrosted seafood mix and cook 1 to 2 minutes, being sure the seafood does not overcook. Add the white wine and butter, cooking until the butter melts, just 30 seconds to 1 minute.

3. Remove the pan from the heat, add the pasta, and toss to combine.

SPINACH ALFREDO LINGUINE with CHICKEN

Creamy Alfredo sauce melds with spinach linguine and chopped spinach for double the spinach power.

½ (16-ounce) package frozen chopped spinach

1 (8-ounce) package Trader Joe's Spinach and Chive Linguine Pasta

1 tablespoon olive oil

1 (16.9-ounce) jar Trader Giotto's Alfredo Pasta Sauce

½ (12-ounce) package Trader Joe's Grilled Chicken Strips

Trader Joe's Grated Parmigiano-Reggiano cheese, as needed (optional)

Yield: 3 servings
Prep Time: 5 minutes
Cook Time: 15 minutes

1. In a small colander, run cold water over the spinach until thawed, 3 to 4 minutes, then squeeze it to remove excess water.

2. Cook the pasta according to the package directions. Drain, rinse with cold water, and toss with the olive oil.

3. In the pot used for the pasta, heat the Alfredo sauce over medium-high heat. Toss in the spinach, stirring to make sure it's well combined with the sauce. Add the chicken and cook until hot.

4. Add the pasta and toss to combine. Top with cheese, if desired.

SPAGHETTI and MEATBALLS

Trader Joe's Flame Broiled Turkey Meatballs add a grilled flavor to this traditional dish.

¼ (16-ounce package) Trader Giotto's Organic Spaghetti

1 tablespoon olive oil

½ (25-ounce) jar Trader Giotto's Organic Tomato Basil Marinara

3 tablespoons unsalted butter, cut into pieces

½ (16-ounce) package frozen Trader Joe's Flame Broiled Turkey Meatballs Fully Cooked

2 to 3 tablespoons Trader Joe's Grated Parmigiano-Reggiano cheese (optional)

Yield: 2 servings
Prep Time: 5 minutes
Cook Time: 15 minutes

1. Cook the spaghetti according to the package directions. Drain and toss with the olive oil.

2. In a medium skillet, heat the marinara sauce over medium-high heat. Once it's bubbling, reduce the heat to low and simmer. Add the butter pieces and stir.

3. Microwave the meatballs according to the package directions. Add the meatballs to the sauce and stir. Simmer for 5 minutes. Remove the pot from the heat, add the pasta, and toss to combine. Top with cheese, if using.

FUSILLI with PESTO, PEAS, and PROSCIUTTO

Because both the pesto and prosciutto are relatively salty, taste the pasta before adding any salt.

½ (16-ounce) package Trader Joe's Organic Fusilli Pasta

½ (16-ounce) bag Trader Joe's Petite Peas

½ (4-ounce) package Trader Joe's Sliced Prosciutto

1 (6.7-ounce) jar Trader Giotto's Pesto alla Genovese (basil pesto)

¼ teaspoon freshly ground black pepper

Yield: 2 servings
Prep Time: 5 minutes
Cook Time: 15 minutes

1. Bring a medium pot of salted water to a boil over high heat. Add the fusilli to the water and cook for 8 minutes. Add the peas to the boiling water with the pasta and cook until the pasta is al dente (see page 193), about 2 minutes longer. Reserve ½ cup of pasta water, then drain the pasta and peas in a colander.

2. Shred the prosciutto into bite-size pieces.

3. Transfer the pasta and peas back to the pot and add the pesto, reserved pasta water, and pepper. Stir constantly to let the pesto incorporate with the pasta and peas. Warm over low heat, as needed. Top with the shredded prosciutto.

ONE-POT SPAGHETTI and MEATBALLS

This one-pot wonder is as simple as can be. To get every last bit of sauce from the jar, add the 2½ cups of water to it, replace the lid, and shake. Then pour the water into the pot.

1 (24-ounce) jar Trader Joe's Roasted Garlic Spaghetti Sauce

2½ cups water

¾ (16-ounce) package Trader Joe's Italian Spaghetti

1 (16-ounce) package frozen Trader Joe's Flame Broiled Turkey Meatballs Fully Cooked, thawed

¼ teaspoon kosher salt

¼ teaspoon freshly ground black pepper

⅓ cup Trader Joe's Parmesan, Romano, and Asiago Blend, for garnish (optional)

Yield: 4 servings
Prep Time: 5 minutes
Cook Time: 30 minutes

1. To a large heavy-duty pot, add the tomato sauce and water. Break the spaghetti in half and add to the pot, along with the meatballs. Season with salt and pepper. Bring the mixture to a boil over medium-high heat.

2. Cover and reduce the heat to medium-low. Stirring occasionally to prevent the pasta from sticking, cook until the spaghetti is tender, 15 to 20 minutes. Garnish with the cheese, if using. Serve.

SPAGHETTI with CHICKEN SAUSAGE and TOMATO SAUCE

A quick, basic tomato sauce should be in everyone's cooking arsenal. The sausage is an easy addition that makes this feel like a full meal.

½ (28-ounce) can Trader Joe's Plum Tomatoes with Basil

2 tablespoons olive oil, divided

1 small or medium onion, diced (see page 192)

½ (12-ounce) package Trader Joe's Sweet Apple Chicken Sausage, sliced into ½-inch rounds

½ teaspoon freshly ground black pepper

1 teaspoon white vinegar or lemon juice

6 ounces Trader Giotto's Organic Spaghetti

Yield: 2 servings
Prep Time: 10 minutes
Cook Time: 40 minutes

1. Pour the tomatoes into a bowl and break the whole tomatoes into 2 to 3 pieces each.

2. Heat 1 tablespoon of oil in a medium skillet over medium heat until shimmering, then add the onion and cook for 30 to 45 seconds, stirring constantly to prevent burning. Add the tomatoes and their liquid, and the sausage, pepper, and vinegar. Bring to a boil, then reduce heat to low, cover the pan, and simmer until the flavors have combined, 20 to 30 minutes.

3. Meanwhile, cook the spaghetti according to the package directions. Drain and toss with the remaining 1 tablespoon of olive oil. Add the pasta to the sauce and toss to combine.

CHAPTER 6

MAIN MEALS

You've had a long day full of sleep-inducing lectures and handed-in assignments. At the end of the night, you crave a good meal that's low on hassle. Well, you're in luck. With step-by-step instructions and Trader Joe's products, whipping up warm homemade meals can be done on the cheap and with ease. There's no need to survive on ramen noodles night after night. Cook chicken thighs in tomatillo salsa and eat them with tortillas, or sauté pork chops and top them with a creamy spinach sauce. A delicious dinner is just minutes away.

FISH TACOS with MANGO SALSA

The sweetness of Trader Joe's Corn and Chile Salsa begs for a fruitlicious pairing like mango.

2 fillets frozen Trader Joe's Panko Breaded Tilapia Fillets

½ mango, diced

½ cup Trader Joe's Corn and Chile Tomato-Less Salsa

4 corn or flour tortillas

cilantro sprigs (optional)

Yield: 4 tacos
Prep Time: 5 minutes
Cook Time: 20 to 25 minutes

1. Preheat the oven to 425°F. Line a rimmed baking sheet with foil.

2. Place the fish fillets on the prepared baking sheet and bake until hot, 20 to 25 minutes.

3. In a small bowl, stir together the mango and corn salsa.

4. Cut the fish into strips. Layer the fish strips onto the tortillas, garnishing with the mango and corn salsa and cilantro sprigs.

CHICKEN MASALA with SWEET POTATOES

Trader Joe's Masala Simmer Sauce is inspired by the typical preparation of chicken tikka masala, which has a tomato base and mild Indian spices.

1 (15-ounce) jar Trader Joe's Masala Simmer Sauce

½ cup water

2 pieces frozen Trader Joe's Boneless Skinless Chicken Thigh Meat

½ teaspoon kosher salt

¼ teaspoon freshly ground black pepper

1 (12-ounce) bag Trader Joe's Sweet Potato Spears or 1 (12-ounce) container Butternut Squash Zig-Zags

1 (18-ounce) package Trader Joe's Indian Style Garlic Flatbread

Yield: 2 servings
Prep Time: 5 minutes
Cook Time: 30 minutes

1. In a medium pot, combine the masala simmer sauce, water, chicken, salt, and pepper. Heat the mixture over high heat until it boils, then cover the pot and reduce the heat to low. Cook for 15 minutes.

2. Meanwhile, coarsely chop the sweet potato into bite-size pieces. Stir the sweet potatoes into the sauce. Cover the pot and cook an additional 15 minutes.

3. Remove the pot from the heat. Cut into the thickest chicken piece to determine it's no longer pink. Serve with flatbread or rice.

TUNA CASSEROLE

This one-skillet wonder is based on a tuna casserole recipe my mom made for me growing up. It continues to be one of my favorite dishes.

1 tablespoon canola oil

celery and onions from 1 (14.5-ounce) container Trader Joe's Mirepoix

½ teaspoon kosher salt

2 Trader Joe's Fire-Roasted Red Peppers, cut into bite-size pieces

2 (5-ounce) cans Trader Joe's Albacore Solid White Tuna in Water

½ cup mayonnaise

½ cup Trader Joe's Japanese-Style Panko Bread Crumbs

Yield: 2 servings
Prep Time: 10 minutes
Cook Time: 25 minutes

1. Preheat the oven to 350°F.

2. In a medium oven-safe skillet, heat the oil over medium-high heat until shimmering. Add the celery and onions and sauté until the vegetables are soft, 4 to 5 minutes.

3. Remove the pan from the heat. Add the salt, peppers, tuna, and mayonnaise, stirring to combine. Top the casserole with bread crumbs. Bake until the tuna is hot throughout, 15 to 20 minutes.

CHICKEN in TOMATILLO SAUCE

This recipe uses two kinds of Trader Joe's tomatillo sauce. The jarred salsa verde is tangier, while the refrigerated autentica version is chunkier.

1 (12-ounce) jar Trader Joe's Salsa Verde

1 (12-ounce) container Trader Joe's Salsa Verde Autentica

2 to 3 pieces frozen Trader Joe's Boneless Skinless Chicken Thigh Meat

½ teaspoon kosher salt

¼ teaspoon freshly ground black pepper

Trader Joe's Handmade Flour Tortillas

Yield: 2 servings
Prep Time: 5 minutes
Cook Time: 30 minutes

1. In a medium pot, add the salsa verde, salsa verde autentica, chicken, salt, and pepper. Stir to combine.

2. Heat the mixture over high heat until the liquid boils. Cover and reduce the heat to low. Simmer until the chicken is cooked through, 25 to 30 minutes. Cut into the thickest chicken piece to determine it's no longer pink.

3. Remove the chicken from the tomatillo sauce and cut it into pieces. Return the chicken to the sauce. Serve with tortillas.

GARLIC BUTTER SHRIMP with QUINOA

Pairing the super-tasty shrimp, butter, and garlic trio with quinoa, a grainlike seed packed with amino acids, protein, and other nutrients, makes this a healthy dinner.

½ (16-ounce) package Trader Joe's Quinoa Duo with Vegetable Melange

3 tablespoons unsalted butter

1 tablespoon Trader Joe's Crushed Garlic

½ teaspoon kosher salt

¼ teaspoon freshly ground black pepper

½ pound Trader Joe's Jumbo Cooked Shrimp (to use raw shrimp, see page 195)

Yield: 2 servings
Prep Time: 5 minutes
Cook Time: 7 minutes

1. Microwave the quinoa and vegetables in a large dish according to the package directions.

2. In a medium skillet over medium-high, melt the butter, then add the garlic, salt, and pepper and cook for just 30 seconds. Add the cooked shrimp and stir to coat it in the sauce just until hot, about 30 seconds.

3. Pour the shrimp and sauce over the quinoa and vegetables.

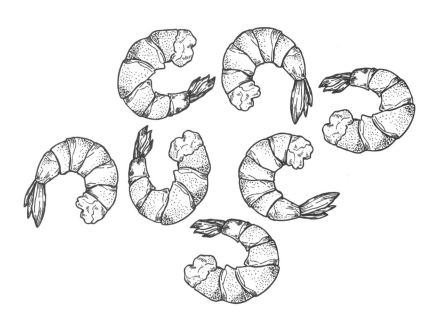

CHICKEN and CHEESE ENCHILADAS

Add a little cayenne pepper into the mix if you want to kick up the spiciness of these enchiladas.

½ (16-ounce) package Trader Joe's Just Chicken White Meat

1 (12-ounce) bottle Trader Joe's Enchilada Sauce, divided

½ teaspoon kosher salt

¼ teaspoon freshly ground black pepper

1½ cups shredded cheese, such as Trader Joe's Fancy Shredded Lite Mexican Blend, divided

½ cup sour cream

4 to 6 whole wheat flour tortillas

Yield: 4 to 6 enchiladas
Prep Time: 15 minutes
Cook Time: 25 minutes

1. Preheat the oven to 400°F. Spray a baking dish with cooking spray.

2. Chop the chicken into very small pieces and place in a medium bowl with three-quarters of the enchilada sauce, the salt, pepper, 1 cup of shredded cheese, and sour cream. Stir to combine the enchilada filling.

3. Spoon the filling down the center of each tortilla, dividing it evenly among the tortillas, and roll the enchiladas up.

4. Arrange the enchiladas in the prepared baking dish. Drizzle the remaining sauce over the enchiladas.

5. Bake until the enchiladas are hot throughout, 20 to 25 minutes. Garnish with the remaining cheese.

MEDITERRANEAN CHICKEN with FETA CHEESE and SUN DRIED TOMATOES

This dish is easy enough to make for yourself on a weekly basis, but flavorful and colorful enough to serve on a special occasion.

1 pound Trader Joe's Organic Free Range Chicken Breast Tenders

½ teaspoon kosher salt

¼ teaspoon freshly ground black pepper

1 tablespoon canola oil

½ cup Trader Joe's Julienne Sliced Sun Dried Tomatoes in Olive Oil, plus 1 tablespoon of the oil

¼ cup pitted kalamata olives

½ cup Trader Joe's Crumbled Feta with Mediterranean Herbs

Yield: 2 servings
Prep Time: 5 minutes
Cook Time: 6 minutes

1. Season the chicken with salt and pepper. In a medium skillet, heat the oil over medium-high heat until shimmering. Add the chicken and sauté until golden on one side, 2 to 3 minutes. Flip the chicken over and cook for 2 to 3 minutes longer. Cut into the thickest piece to determine it's no longer pink.

2. In a small bowl, stir the sun dried tomatoes and accompanying oil with the olives and feta to combine.

3. Transfer the chicken to a serving plate and top with the feta mixture.

PORK CHOPS in CREAMY SPINACH SAUCE

This recipe uses Frenched pork chops, which are rib chops from which the meat and fat have been trimmed from the end of the bone.

1 package (about 1 pound) Trader Joe's Bone-in Frenched Center Cut Pork Chops

½ teaspoon kosher salt

¼ teaspoon freshly ground black pepper

1 tablespoon canola oil

½ (8.8-ounce) container frozen Trader Joe's Creamy Spinach and Artichoke Dip

2 tablespoons heavy cream

Yield: 2 servings
Prep Time: 5 minutes
Cook Time: 12 minutes

1. Pat the pork chops dry with a paper towel and season them with salt and pepper.

2. In a large heavy skillet, heat the oil over medium-high heat until shimmering. Carefully add the pork chops and sauté until browned and golden on each side, about 4 minutes per side.

3. Remove the pan from the heat and transfer the pork chops to a cutting board. Cut into one of the pork chops to determine it's no longer pink. Cover loosely with foil.

4. In a microwave-safe dish, add the spinach dip, cheese-side up. Microwave on high for 2 minutes.

5. Stir the heavy cream into the spinach dip and microwave on high for 2 minutes longer. Transfer the pork chops to plates and pour the spinach sauce over the meat.

ASIAN MEATBALLS in PEANUT SAUCE

These Asian-flavored pork meatballs are paired with thin capellini noodles and tossed in a Thai vinaigrette.

½ pound ground pork

½ (8-ounce) can water chestnuts, finely chopped

1 tablespoon minced ginger

1 large egg

½ teaspoon kosher salt

¼ teaspoon freshly ground black pepper

¼ cup Trader Joe's Japanese-Style Panko Bread Crumbs

½ (16-ounce) package Trader Joe's Italian Capellini

½ cup Trader Joe's Asian Style Spicy Peanut Vinaigrette, plus more if needed

½ cup chopped cilantro

¼ cup chopped scallions

Yield: 3 servings
Prep Time: 15 minutes
Cook Time: 20 minutes

1. Preheat the oven to 425°F. Spray a rimmed baking sheet with cooking spray.

2. In a large bowl, combine the ground pork, water chestnuts, ginger, egg, salt, pepper, and bread crumbs with your hands.

3. Roll about 1 tablespoon of the meat mixture into meatballs, one at a time, and place on the prepared baking sheet. Bake until cooked through, 12 to 15 minutes. Cut into a meatball to determine that it's no longer pink.

4. Meanwhile, cook the capellini according to the package directions. Drain the pasta in a colander and rinse to cool the noodles. To a large bowl, add the vinaigrette, cilantro, and scallions. To the bowl, add the capellini, tossing to combine. Taste, adding more vinaigrette if needed. Top the pasta with the meatballs to serve.

SOYAKI STEAK

Trader Joe's Island Soyaki includes pineapple juice, which contains bromelain, a natural enzyme known to tenderize meat.

1 Trader Joe's Butcher Shop Boneless Beef Rib Eye Steak (about 1 pound)
1 cup Trader Joe's Island Soyaki
kosher salt and freshly ground black pepper

Yield: 2 servings
Prep Time: 5 minutes active, plus 1 hour for marinating
Cook Time: 6 to 10 minutes, depending on desired doneness of steak

1. In a shallow dish, cover the steak with the Soyaki. Marinate for at least 1 hour in the refrigerator.

2. Remove the steak from the marinade and discard the marinade. Dab the steak with a paper towel to remove the marinade.

3. Preheat the oven's broiler. Line a rimmed baking sheet with foil.

4. Place the steak on the prepared baking sheet and season it with salt and pepper. Cook the steak under the broiler for 2 to 3 minutes per side, until it reaches your desired doneness (see page 193). You may need to make a cut into the center of the steak to determine its doneness.

5. Remove the steak from the oven, transfer to a cutting board, and cover with a piece of foil. Let the steak rest for 5 minutes before slicing and serving.

BEEF STROGANOFF WANNABE

Trader Joe's Condensed Cream of Portabella Soup infuses beefy noodles with that earthy mushroom taste.

1 (10-ounce) package sliced white mushrooms

½ tablespoon canola oil

½ (16-ounce) package Trader Joe's Italian Fusilli

½ (16-ounce) package Trader Joe's Traditional Pot Roast, cut into bite-size pieces

1 (11-ounce) box Trader Joe's Condensed Cream of Portabella Mushroom Soup

½ teaspoon kosher salt

½ teaspoon freshly ground black pepper

1 cup sour cream

2 tablespoons chopped chives (optional)

Yield: 2 servings
Prep Time: 5 minutes
Cook Time: 18 minutes

1. Cut the larger mushrooms in half so all the slices are similar in size.

2. In a medium skillet, heat the oil over medium-high heat until shimmering. Add the mushrooms and cook until softened, about 10 minutes, stirring occasionally.

3. Cook the fusilli according to the package directions and drain.

4. Increase the heat to high and add the pot roast pieces to the mushrooms, mixing the mushrooms and beef together and cooking just 1 minute. Add the portabella soup, salt, and pepper. Cook until the sauce is bubbling, 2 to 3 minutes, stirring occasionally.

5. Remove from the heat and stir in the sour cream. Toss with the pasta. Garnish with chives, if using.

BACON CHEESEBURGER

This is a good basic hamburger recipe—you're free to use any toppings you like.

1 (1-pound) package Trader Joe's Organic Ground Beef

2 teaspoons Trader Joe's Everyday Seasoning with Grinder

2 teaspoons canola oil

4 slices Trader Joe's Fully Cooked Uncured Bacon (about 4 slices)

4 Trader Joe's Honey Wheat Hamburger Buns

4 slices American cheese or your favorite kind

OPTIONAL CONDIMENTS AND TOPPINGS:
ketchup, mustard, lettuce, tomato, avocado, onions, salsa

Yield: 4 burgers
Prep Time: 10 minutes
Cook Time: 6 minutes

1. Place the ground beef in a medium bowl and grind the everyday seasoning onto the meat and combine. Mold the meat into 4 patties.

2. In a medium skillet, heat the oil over medium-high heat until shimmering. Add the hamburger patties to the pan and cook until both burger sides are browned and have reached the desired doneness in the center (see page 193), about 3 minutes on each side, making sure to press the burgers down with a spatula when flipping them.

3. Meanwhile, arrange the bacon slices between layers of paper towels in a small microwave-safe dish. Microwave on high until crispy, 30 to 45 seconds. Warm the buns in the microwave.

4. Top each burger with a slice of cheese. Transfer the cheeseburgers to the buns and top with the bacon and other desired condiments.

SLOPPY JOES

When I was a kid, sloppy joes were my go-to birthday meal request.

1 teaspoon canola oil

1 pound Trader Joe's Butcher Shop Ground Beef 80/20

½ teaspoon kosher salt

¼ teaspoon freshly ground black pepper

½ cup ketchup

2 tablespoons yellow mustard

2 tablespoons honey

3 to 4 Trader Joe's Honey Wheat Hamburger Buns

Yield: 3 to 4 servings
Prep Time: 5 minutes
Cook Time: 10 minutes

1. In a medium skillet, heat the oil over medium-high heat until shimmering. Add the ground beef, salt, and pepper, stirring every couple of minutes to break up the meat. Sauté the meat until fully cooked, 6 to 7 minutes.

2. Take the pan off the heat. Push the cooked meat to one side of the pan and remove and discard most of the fat.

3. Stir the ketchup, mustard, and honey into the beef and heat the mixture over medium-high heat until the beef is hot and combined with the sauce. Remove from the heat and cover, to keep hot. Microwave the buns until warm. Pile the meat mixture onto the buns.

Note: The term "80/20" refers to the percentage of fat contained in the meat: 80/20 beef has 20 percent fat and is considered 80 percent lean.

TOSTADAS

Freshly fried to a golden crisp, tostadas are crunchy, slightly greasy (in a good way), and downright delicious.

½ (12-ounce) package Trader Joe's Carnitas

½ (15-ounce) can Trader Joe's Refried Black Beans with Jalapeño Peppers

½ (8-ounce) package Trader Joe's Shredded Pepper Jack Cheese Blend

canola oil, as needed

3 flour tortillas

½ (16-ounce) container Trader José's Guacamole Topped with Spicy Pico de Gallo

OPTIONAL TOPPINGS: chopped tomatoes, shredded lettuce, sour cream, salsa

Yield: 3 tostadas
Prep Time: 5 minutes
Cook Time: 12 minutes

1. Line a plate with a paper towel.

2. In a large bowl combine the carnitas and refried beans and microwave on high for 2 to 3 minutes. Remove from the microwave and top with the cheese.

3. In a large skillet, heat 1 inch of oil over high heat until shimmering. Add 1 tortilla and fry until golden, about 2 minutes per side. Transfer to the prepared plate to drain. Repeat with the remaining tortillas.

4. Layer the tostadas with the hot meat and bean mixture and top with guacamole and pico de gallo and other desired toppings.

MEATLOAF MUFFINS

Making meatloaf into muffins not only makes it cuter, it greatly shortens the cooking time.

½ cup Trader Joe's Cheese and Garlic Croutons

¾ pound Trader Joe's Butcher Shop Ground Beef 96/4

1 cup frozen Trader Joe's Fire Roasted Bell Pepper and Onions, thawed

1 teaspoon kosher salt

½ teaspoon freshly ground black pepper

1 large egg

2 tablespoons ketchup

½ cup Trader Joe's Sweet and Spicy Mustard

Yield: 8 meatloaf muffins
Prep Time: 20 minutes
Cook Time: 30 minutes

1. Preheat the oven to 350°F. Spray 8 muffin cups with cooking spray.

2. Seal the croutons in a plastic bag and pound into crumbs. In a large bowl, mix the crumbs, ground beef, pepper and onions, salt, pepper, egg, and ketchup.

3. Pack the meat mixture into as many prepared muffin cups as possible until almost full but not overflowing. Pour water into any empty cups to prevent scorching. Bake for 15 minutes. Remove the pan from the oven and glaze each meat loaf with the mustard.

4. Return the pan to the oven and cook for an additional 15 minutes. Cut into one meatloaf muffin to make sure it's no longer pink. Cool for a few minutes.

CHAPTER 7

VEGETARIAN MAIN MEALS

Even if you're a massive carnivore, vegetarian meals should be slowly woven into your diet (and take this from a total carnivore herself). One good reason is that meat—even with Trader Joe's meat at drastically affordable prices—is more expensive to consume. Meals with veggies, beans, and/or soy products are going to be more affordable.

TERIYAKI TOFU with BABY BROCCOLI

Tofu doesn't have a ton of flavor, which is why it's good to let it marinate in Trader Joe San Soyaki to give it a great taste for this filling vegan meal.

½ (14-ounce) package Trader Joe's Firm Organic Tofu, cut into ½-inch cubes

½ (21-ounce) bottle Trader Joe San Soyaki

1 tablespoon canola oil

1 (8-ounce) package Trader Joe's Organic Baby Broccoli, cut into 1-inch pieces

1 Trader Joe's Fire Roasted Red Pepper (from a jar), cut into bite-size pieces

1 (10-ounce) package frozen Trader Joe's Organic Jasmine Rice

Yield: 2 servings
Prep Time: 10 minutes active, plus 30 minutes for marinating
Cook Time: 10 minutes

1. In a medium bowl, cover the tofu cubes with the Soyaki and let marinate for at least 30 minutes. When ready to use, drain the tofu, reserving ⅓ cup of the marinade.

2. Heat the oil in a large skillet over medium heat until shimmering. Add the broccoli, red pepper, and tofu and sauté about 5 minutes. Add the reserved marinade and cook until the broccoli is fully cooked, about 5 minutes, stirring occasionally.

3. Microwave the rice according to the package directions. Scoop the rice into bowls and top with the tofu mixture.

TAQUITO CASSEROLE

Trader Joe's thin black bean–stuffed taquitos are piled on top of each other and blended with sour cream, salsa, and cheese.

1 (16-ounce) package Trader José's Black Bean and Cheese Taquitos (12 pieces)

1 cup sour cream

¾ cup Trader Joe's Organic Tomatillo and Roasted Yellow Chili Salsa

½ (11.5-ounce) jar Trader Joe's Queso Cheese Dip

Yield: 2 servings
Prep Time: 10 minutes
Cook Time: 25 minutes

1. Preheat the oven to 400°F. In a small baking dish, lay half the taquitos side by side.

2. In a small bowl, mix the sour cream and salsa together. Pour the sauce over the taquitos and layer the remaining taquitos on top. Top the second layer of taquitos with the queso dip.

3. Bake until hot, 20 to 25 minutes.

TACO TIME

This has all the ingredients that make for a vegetarian version of a classic taco, including Trader Joe's Beef-less Ground Beef.

1 (12-ounce) package Trader Joe's Beef-less Ground Beef

½ (16-ounce) can Trader Joe's Vegetarian Refried Pinto Beans

½ cup Trader Joe's Fancy Shredded Mexican Cheese Blend

½ (5.5-ounce) package Trader José's Taco Shells

¼ cup Trader Joe's Salsa Autentica, for garnish

1 cup shredded lettuce, for garnish

2 Roma tomatoes, chopped, for garnish

Yield: 2 servings
Prep Time: 5 minutes
Cook Time: 5 minutes

1. To a medium microwave-safe dish, add the beef-less ground beef and pinto beans. Microwave on high until hot, 2 to 3 minutes, stirring halfway through. Top with the cheese and microwave on high until melted, about 30 seconds.

2. Pile the mixture into the taco shells. Garnish with the salsa, lettuce, and tomatoes.

CURRIED CAULIFLOWER

I've long thought that cauliflower is an underappreciated vegetable. Its subtle flavor works well with the greater intensity of the dairy-free Curry Simmer Sauce.

2 (12-ounce) bags cauliflower florets

1 (15-ounce) jar Trader Joe's Curry Simmer Sauce

1 (10-ounce) package frozen Trader Joe's Organic Brown Rice

Yield: 2 servings
Prep Time: 5 minutes
Cook Time: 6 minutes

1. Snip off the top corners of the cauliflower packets and microwave on high for 1 minute. In a large microwave-safe dish, place the curry sauce and the cauliflower and microwave on high until hot, about 2 to 3 minutes, stirring halfway through.

2. Cook the rice in the microwave according to the package directions.

3. Stir the rice into the cauliflower and curry sauce.

STUFFED BAKED POTATOES

Don't let the long cooking time in this recipe scare you—all of it is unattended. Just pop the potatoes into the oven and let it do all the work.

2 russet potatoes

½ (8.8-ounce) container frozen Trader Joe's Creamy Spinach and Artichoke Dip

1 tablespoon unsalted butter

kosher salt and freshly ground black pepper

Yield: 2 servings
Prep Time: 10 minutes
Cook Time: 65 minutes

1. Preheat the oven to 400°F.

2. Using a fork, poke numerous holes into the potatoes and place them on a rimmed baking sheet. Bake until a knife can be inserted into a potato without any resistance, about 1 hour. Let the potatoes cool for about 10 minutes.

3. Meanwhile, in a microwave-safe dish, place the dip, cheese-side up. Microwave on high for 2 minutes. Stir and cook 2 minutes longer.

4. Slice halfway through the center of each potato, lengthwise. Add ½ tablespoon butter to each potato and season to taste with salt and pepper. Pour the hot dip over each potato.

BRIE and BUTTERNUT SQUASH QUESADILLAS

The rich creaminess of the brie combined with the butternut squash mashed with brown sugar harnesses the flavors of fall.

1 (12-ounce) bag Trader Joe's Cut Butternut Squash

1 tablespoon brown sugar

¼ teaspoon kosher salt

¼ teaspoon freshly ground black pepper

½ wedge Trader Joe's Supreme Brie

2 whole wheat flour tortillas

1 tablespoon canola oil, plus more as needed

Yield: 2 quesadillas
Prep Time: 5 minutes
Cook Time: 12 minutes

1. Cook the butternut squash according to the package directions. Transfer to a small bowl and mash with the brown sugar, salt, and pepper.

2. Spread a little brie on each tortilla. Spread the squash mixture on half of each tortilla, then fold the tortillas in half.

3. In a medium nonstick skillet, heat 1 tablespoon of oil over medium-high heat until shimmering. Add 1 tortilla, cooking until each side is golden, about 3 minutes per side. Repeat with the remaining tortilla, adding more oil as needed.

4. Remove the quesadillas from the pan and cut each one into 4 wedges.

ZUCCHINI and POLENTA BAKE

Who needs a grill for smoky vegetables when you can open a bag of Trader Giotto's Misto alla Griglia (grilled marinated eggplant and zucchini)?

½ (16-ounce) bag frozen Trader Giotto's Misto alla Griglia

½ (18-ounce) tube Trader Joe's Organic Polenta

1 cup Trader Giotto's Traditional Fresh Ricotta

1½ cups Trader Giotto's Organic Tomato Basil Marinara

Yield: 2 servings
Prep Time: 5 minutes
Cook Time: 22 minutes

1. Preheat the oven to 350°F.

2. In a microwave-safe dish, microwave the eggplant and zucchini on high for 2 minutes.

3. Cut the polenta into about 8 (½-inch) slices and arrange them in a baking dish, then add the eggplant and zucchini slices on top.

4. In a small bowl, stir together the ricotta and marinara sauce to combine. Pour the sauce over the vegetables and polenta. Bake until hot, about 20 minutes.

RICE and BLACK BEANS

Rice and beans are cheap, tasty, and filled with protein.

1 (10-ounce) pouch frozen Trader Joe's Brown Rice

1 (15.5-ounce) can Trader Joe's Black Beans

½ (16-ounce) container Trader José's Guacamole Topped with Spicy Pico de Gallo

½ cup sour cream

2 scallions, chopped

Yield: 2 servings
Prep Time: 5 minutes
Cook Time: 5 minutes

1. Cook the rice in the microwave according to the package directions.

2. In a large microwave-safe dish, place the cooked rice and stir in the black beans. Microwave on high until hot, 2 to 3 minutes, stirring halfway through.

3. Stir in the guacamole and pico de gallo. Top with dollops of sour cream and scallions.

OLIVE, RED PEPPER, and ARUGULA PIZZA

Let your creativity go wild to top this pizza with whatever you have in the fridge. No rolling pin required, just your hands are needed to stretch the dough.

flour, as needed

1 ball Trader Joe's Pizza Dough, at room temperature

½ (10-ounce) container Trader Joe's Pizza Sauce

½ (8-ounce) Trader Joe's Fresh Mozzarella ball, grated

1 red pepper from Trader Joe's Fire-Roasted Red Peppers, cut into slices

¼ cup pitted kalamata olives, cut in half

1 handful arugula

Yield: 2 servings
Prep Time: 10 minutes
Cook Time: 16 minutes

1. Preheat the oven to 450°F.

2. Sprinkle 1 to 2 tablespoons of flour onto a cutting board, flouring the cutting board and your hands. Remove the pizza dough from the plastic. Slowly, stretch the dough on the back of your knuckles, rotating the dough and stretching it out into a circular shape. When the dough is stretched out to about 1 foot in diameter, place it on the cutting board and stretch it even more, using your fingertips.

3. Place the dough directly onto one of the oven racks. Bake until the bottom of the crust is cooked through, about 4 minutes. Using tongs, remove from the oven and place on the cutting board with the bottom face-up.

4. Spread the pizza sauce onto the dough and top with mozzarella slices. Add the red pepper slices and olives on top of the cheese.

5. Place the pizza in the oven, directly on the wire rack. Bake until the crust is fully cooked and crisp and the cheese has melted, about 12 minutes longer. Using tongs, carefully remove the pizza from the oven.

6. Spread the arugula on top and cut into pieces.

VEGETABLE FRIED RICE

The key to good vegetable fried rice is to make sure the frozen rice is fully thawed so each rice grain can get coated with oil and "fried" during the cooking process.

2 large eggs

1 tablespoon water

1 tablespoon plus 1 teaspoon canola oil, divided

1 (12-ounce) bag sugar snap peas

½ (16-ounce) bag frozen Trader Joe's Vegetable Fried Rice, thawed

½ (7-ounce) package Trader Joe's Organic Baked Tofu Savory Flavor, cubed

2 scallions, chopped

Yield: 2 servings
Prep Time: 5 minutes
Cook Time: 10 minutes

1. Crack the eggs into a small bowl. Add the water and use a fork or whisk to combine.

2. In a medium nonstick skillet, heat 1 teaspoon oil over medium-high heat until shimmering. Add the eggs and use a spatula to constantly move the eggs from the side of the skillet into the center until they're fully cooked, 2 to 3 minutes. Transfer the eggs to a clean bowl and set aside.

3. Microwave the sugar snap peas in their bag on high for 2 minutes.

4. Wipe the skillet clean, then heat the remaining 1 teaspoon of oil over high heat until shimmering. Add the vegetable fried rice. Cook until hot, 2 to 3 minutes, stirring constantly. Add the sugar snap peas along with the tofu. Stir to combine and cook until hot, 1 to 2 minutes.

5. Stir in the reserved scrambled eggs and remove from the heat. Sprinkle with scallions.

The I ♥ **TRADER JOE'S®** COLLEGE COOKBOOK

MICROWAVE MAIN MEALS

These recipes prove that even if you're equipped with just a microwave and a tiny fridge in your dorm, you can still cook tasty meals. Armed with Trader Joe's ingredients and these recipes, there's no excuse not to whip up a feast. Also, Trader Joe's frozen goods are of such high quality they don't have that frozen food taste that others suffer from. No one will ever be the wiser that the entire meal was made in the microwave.

TAMALE-ENCHILADA CASSEROLE

Pairing tamales with cheese and enchilada sauce creates a delicious treat.

1 (10-ounce) package Trader José's Handcrafted Chicken and Cheese Tamales

1 (10-ounce) package Trader José's Handcrafted Cheese and Green Chile Tamales

½ (12-ounce) bottle Trader Joe's Enchilada Sauce

1 cup shredded cheese, like Trader Joe's Fancy Shredded Lite Mexican Blend

Yield: 2 servings
Prep Time: 2 minutes
Cook Time: 10 minutes

1. Remove the plastic from the tamales and microwave on high until warm, 2 to 3 minutes. Carefully remove the tamales from the corn husks.

2. In a long microwave-safe dish, arrange the tamales in a row. Cut each one in half for quicker heating. Pour the enchilada sauce over the tamales and top with the cheese.

3. Microwave the casserole on high until hot, 3 to 4 more minutes.

BLACK PEPPER SHRIMP with FRIED RICE

To add a splash of spiciness to this microwave dish, douse with Trader Joe's Sriracha Sauce.

½ (16-ounce) bag frozen Trader Joe's Vegetable Fried Rice

½ (16-ounce) bag frozen Trader Joe's Jumbo Cooked Shrimp, thawed (to use raw shrimp, see page 195)

½ teaspoon freshly ground black pepper

Yield: 2 servings
Prep Time: 1 minute
Cook Time: 5 minutes

1. In a microwave-safe dish, microwave the fried rice on high until hot, 2 to 3 minutes.

2. In another microwave-safe dish, stir together the shrimp and black pepper. Microwave on high until just warm, about 30 seconds. Top the fried rice with the black pepper shrimp.

VEGGIE RISOTTO with SHRIMP

Making risotto, normally a very time-consuming process, has already been tackled thanks to Trader Joe's.

⅓ (14-ounce) bag frozen Trader Joe's Bean So Green

1 (16-ounce) package frozen Trader Joe's Asparagus Risotto

⅓ (16-ounce) bag Trader Joe's Jumbo Cooked Shrimp (to use raw shrimp, see page 195)

2 tablespoons Trader Joe's Grated Parmigiano-Reggiano cheese (optional)

Yield: 2 servings
Prep Time: 5 minutes
Cook Time: 5 minutes

1. Cut the green beans from the vegetable mix into bite-size pieces. Transfer the risotto to a microwave-safe dish and add the vegetable mix on top of it. Microwave on high until hot, 3 to 4 minutes.

2. In another microwave-safe dish, microwave the shrimp until just warm, about 30 seconds.

3. Add the shrimp to the risotto and top with the cheese, if using.

CHICKEN PARMESAN STRIPS

A simple take on a comfort food classic.

1 (12-ounce) package Trader Joe's Chicken Tenders with Panko Bread Crumbs

1 cup Trader Giotto's Organic Tomato Basil Marinara

2 to 3 slices part-skim mozzarella cheese

2 tablespoons Trader Joe's Grated Parmigiano-Reggiano cheese

Yield: 2 servings
Prep Time: 1 minute
Cook Time: 5 minutes

1. Pierce a few holes in the plastic film over the chicken tenders. Microwave on high until mostly warm, about 2 minutes, then transfer the chicken to a plate. Cover with the marinara sauce and top with the mozzarella and Parmigiano-Reggiano.

2. Microwave on high until hot, 2 to 3 minutes.

SPAGHETTI MEETS MAC and CHEESE

By using Trader Joe's ingredients, this delicious meal is accomplished in only 10 minutes.

1 (14-ounce) box frozen Joe's Diner Mac 'n Cheese

1 (12-ounce) box frozen Trader Joe's "Just Sauce" Turkey Bolognese

1 teaspoon dried oregano (optional)

Yield: 2 servings
Prep Time: 1 minute
Cook Time: 10 minutes

1. Pierce a few holes in the plastic film over the mac and cheese. Microwave for 5 minutes.

2. Microwave the Bolognese sauce on low power for 2 to 3 minutes. Then microwave on high power until the Bolognese is hot throughout, about 3 minutes.

3. Transfer the hot mac and cheese to a medium bowl. Add the oregano, if using, and stir in about three-quarters of the Bolognese sauce. Reserve the remaining sauce for another use.

CARNE ASADA POLENTA "LASAGNA"

Instead of using strips of pasta, this dish layers polenta with cheese, mushrooms, and beef.

1½ cups Trader Joe's Traditional Fresh Ricotta

2 tablespoons Trader Joe's Condensed Cream of Portabella Mushroom Soup

½ (12-ounce) package frozen Trader Joe's Carne Asada (seasoned beef sirloin)

2 scallions, chopped

½ (18-ounce) tube Trader Joe's Organic Polenta

Yield: 2 servings
Prep Time: 10 minutes
Cook Time: 5 minutes

1. In a small bowl, stir together the ricotta, soup, carne asada, and scallions.

2. Cut the polenta into rounds about ¼ inch thick. In a medium microwave-safe dish, make one layer of polenta using 5 to 6 slices and top with half of the ricotta mixture.

3. Add another layer of polenta, using the remaining 5 to 6 slices. Top with the remaining ricotta mixture, smoothing it over the polenta slices.

4. Microwave until hot, 5 to 6 minutes.

BEEF FAJITAS with GUACAMOLE and PICO DE GALLO

Trader José's Guacamole topped with Spicy Pico de Gallo is a two-for-one deal, offering creamy guacamole and spicy salsa all in one container.

½ (14-ounce) bag frozen Trader Joe's Fire Roasted Bell Pepper and Onions

½ (12-ounce) package frozen Trader Joe's Carne Asada (seasoned beef sirloin)

1½ teaspoons Trader Joe's Taco Seasoning Mix

4 whole wheat flour tortillas

½ (16-ounce) container Trader José's Guacamole topped with Spicy Pico de Gallo

Yield: 4 fajitas
Prep Time: 1 minute
Cook Time: 5 minutes

1. In a microwave-safe dish, combine the bell pepper, onions, and carne asada. Microwave on high until hot, about 3 minutes. Sprinkle the taco seasoning on top and stir.

2. Briefly microwave the tortillas until hot, 10 to 15 seconds. Divide the meat and vegetable mixture among the tortillas and top with the guacamole and pico de gallo.

STUFFED RED PEPPERS with CHICKEN and ORZO

This meal is quick and delicious and tastes like it took a long time to assemble, instead of just minutes.

1 (18-ounce) package Trader Joe's Greek Style Chicken with Orzo, Spinach and Feta Cheese

1 (24-ounce) jar Trader Joe's Roasted Red Peppers

¾ cup Trader Joe's Crumbled Feta with Mediterranean Herbs

Yield: 2 servings
Prep Time: 5 minutes
Cook Time: 5 minutes

1. Cut the chicken and olives from the Greek Style Chicken into bite-size pieces. Mix the ingredients together.

2. Lay the peppers in a microwave-safe dish. Using a spoon, fill each pepper with the orzo mixture. Microwave on high until hot, 2 to 3 minutes.

3. Crumble the feta on top of the peppers and microwave again until the cheese is melted, 30 seconds to 1 minute.

PENNE MEATBALLS with ARRABBIATA SAUCE

Arrabbiata *translates to "angry" in Italian, so the name of this sauce comes from the heat of chile peppers.*

1 (16-ounce) bag frozen Authentic Italian Trader Joe's Penne Arrabbiata

1 (16-ounce) package frozen Trader Joe's Flame Broiled Turkey Meatballs Fully Cooked

¼ cup Trader Joe's Grated Parmigiano-Reggiano cheese, for garnish

Yield: 4 servings
Prep Time: 1 minute
Cook Time: 10 minutes

1. Microwave the penne according to the package directions. Set aside.

2. In a medium microwave-safe dish, microwave the meatballs on high for 3 to 5 minutes, until the meatballs are fully heated.

3. Open the bag of pasta and add to a platter. Top with the meatballs and garnish with the cheese.

TORTILLA CHILI CHEESE DOGS

When you're low on time between classes and just want a quick bite to eat, turn to this chili and cheese hot dog goodness.

⅓ (15-ounce) can Trader Joe's Turkey Chili

¼ (11.5-ounce) jar Trader Joe's Queso Cheese Dip

4 Trader Joe's All Natural Uncured All-Beef Hot Dogs

4 whole wheat flour tortillas

Yield: 4 hot dogs
Prep Time: 1 minute
Cook Time: 5 minutes

1. Pour the chili into a bowl and top with the queso dip. Microwave on high, stirring halfway through, until hot, 3 to 4 minutes.

2. Wrap the hot dogs in paper towels and microwave on high until hot, up to 1 minute.

3. Briefly microwave the tortillas until warm, 10 to 15 seconds. Lay the tortillas on a cutting board and add a hot dog to the middle of each one. Spoon the chili-queso mixture over each hot dog until covered.

4. Wrap the tortillas burrito-style, folding up the bottom edge first and then rolling the hot dog in the tortilla so the chili doesn't slip out.

GREEN CHILE SHEPHERD'S PIE

Shepherd's pie is one of my favorite meals. For a Southwestern spin, the mashed potatoes are combined with green chiles and melty cheese.

½ (20-ounce) package Trader Joe's Party Size Mini Meatballs

½ (28-ounce) package frozen Trader Joe's Mashed Potatoes (about 25 medallions)

½ (16-ounce) bag frozen Trader Joe's Roasted Corn

1 (4-ounce) can Trader Joe's Fire Roasted Diced Green Chiles

½ cup Trader Joe's Fancy Shredded Mexican Cheese

Yield: 2 servings
Prep Time: 5 minutes
Cook Time: 10 minutes

1. Cut the meatballs in half and arrange them in a microwave-safe dish. Microwave according to the package directions.

2. In two separate dishes, microwave the potatoes and the corn on high until warm, just 2 to 3 minutes. Layer the corn on top of the meatballs.

3. Mix the chiles into the mashed potatoes, then layer them on top of the corn. Top with a layer of cheese and microwave on high until hot, 2 to 3 minutes.

FISH AND BROCCOLI DINNER

Who needs an oven to make a healthy fish dinner? Thin pieces of fish can be easily steamed, courtesy of the microwave.

2 thin fish fillets, such as frozen Trader Joe's Farm Raised Tilapia Fillets, thawed (aim for ½-inch thickness)

1 tablespoon water

1 tablespoon olive oil

¼ teaspoon kosher salt

Trader Joe's Everything But the Elote Seasoning Blend, as needed

1 (12-ounce) package Trader Joe's Broccoli Florets

3 tablespoons Trader Joe's Pub Cheese

Yield: 2 servings
Prep Time: 5 minutes
Cook Time: 5 minutes

1. To an 8 x 8-inch baking dish, add the fish fillets and water. Drizzle with the oil. Season the fish with the salt and sprinkle it with the seasoning blend. Cover the fish with plastic wrap and poke a small hole in the center of the plastic wrap.

2. Microwave the fish on high for 2½ minutes. Using a fork, check whether the center of the fish flakes easily and is opaque. If not, return it to the microwave in 30-second intervals until done.

3. Next, add the broccoli to the microwave, and cook according to the package directions. Divide the fish and broccoli between 2 serving plates.

4. Add the pub cheese to a small microwave-safe bowl along with a splash of water. Heat just until melted, 15 to 30 seconds. Drizzle the cheese sauce over the broccoli and serve.

CHAPTER 9

SIMPLE SIDES

Give vegetables a chance. You know you want to. And, trust me on this, don't judge veggies by the wilted, soggy ones they serve at the cafeteria. Trader Joe's super-fresh vegetables are usually prewashed, prechopped, and, in a lot of cases, can be cooked in the plastic pouch you buy them in.

There's no reason not to add these babies into your diet in a way that's tasty. In these recipes, broccoli is tossed with olive oil and dried cherries, corn on the cob is slathered with cheese, and carrots are glazed with honey. Also, check out Rice and Vermicelli and Pesto-Roasted Potatoes—both potatoes and rice are cheap ways to get creative with side dishes.

If you're overwhelmed at the thought of cooking a side dish at the same time as a main dish to serve it with, don't fret. These recipes are simple to put together and don't require much multitasking.

HEARTS of PALM with MANGO and ONION

Hearts of palm are exactly what they sound like—a vegetable harvested from the inner core of a certain type of palm tree.

1 (14.5-ounce) package Trader Joe's Hearts of Palm, drained and rinsed

1 mango

¼ cup diced red onion (see page 192)

2 teaspoons olive oil

kosher salt and freshly ground black pepper

Yield: 2 servings
Prep Time: 10 minutes
Cook Time: none

1. Cut each heart of palm into 1-inch pieces. Place in a small bowl. Dice the mango and add it to the bowl, along with the red onion and olive oil. Season to taste with salt and pepper.

2. Using a spoon, mix all the ingredients together to combine.

ROASTED TOMATOES

This vegan recipe for roasted cherry tomatoes is amazingly easy. All you do is season and shove in the oven to let it work its roasting magic.

2 (16-ounce) containers cherry tomatoes

1 tablespoon olive oil

½ teaspoon kosher salt

¼ teaspoon freshly ground black pepper

Yield: 2 servings
Prep Time: 5 minutes
Cook Time: 30 minutes

1. Preheat the oven to 400°F. Line a rimmed baking sheet with foil.

2. Spread the tomatoes on the prepared baking sheet. Drizzle with the olive oil and sprinkle with the salt and pepper. Toss the tomatoes to coat in the oil and seasonings.

3. Bake the tomatoes until crinkly and roasted, 25 to 30 minutes, stirring just once halfway through the cooking time.

ASPARAGUS with AIOLI

Asparagus doesn't require much enhancement, but dipping it into a flavorful aioli adds a little excitement.

1 (12-ounce) package asparagus

kosher salt and freshly ground black pepper

squeeze of lemon

2 tablespoons Trader Joe's Aioli Garlic Mustard Sauce

Yield: 2 servings
Prep Time: 5 minutes
Cook Time: 2 minutes

1. Bring a medium pot three-quarters full of salted water to a boil over high heat.

2. To trim the asparagus, bend the bottom part of the asparagus, 1 to 2 inches from the bottom, and the stalk will snap at the point where tender meets tough. Add the asparagus and cook briefly until tender, just 1 to 2 minutes. Transfer the asparagus to a plate.

3. Sprinkle the asparagus with salt, pepper, and a squeeze of lemon juice. Serve with the aioli as a dipping sauce.

PARMESAN and BREAD CRUMB–CRUSTED TOMATOES

I have yet to serve these tomatoes to anyone who doesn't immediately devour them and ask for the recipe.

2 medium tomatoes

2 tablespoons Trader Joe's Japanese-Style Panko Bread Crumbs

1½ tablespoons Trader Joe's Grated Parmigiano-Reggiano cheese, plus extra for topping

2 tablespoons olive oil

¼ teaspoon kosher salt

Yield: 2 servings
Prep Time: 5 minutes
Cook Time: 10 minutes

1. Preheat the oven to 400°F. Line a rimmed baking sheet with foil.

2. Cut the tomatoes into ½-inch slices, 4 or 5 slices per tomato. Transfer the slices to the prepared baking sheet.

3. In a small bowl, combine the bread crumbs, cheese, olive oil, and salt. Divide the mixture among the tomato slices, mounding it on top of each one. Sprinkle with additional cheese.

4. Bake until the tomatoes are soft and the crust is crispy, 8 to 10 minutes.

BEETS with MINT GREMOLATA

I've converted many beet haters with this sweet, earthy vegan recipe.

1 teaspoon grated lemon zest

¼ teaspoon Trader Joe's Crushed Garlic

2 tablespoons chopped mint

juice of ½ lemon

1 tablespoon olive oil

kosher salt and freshly ground black pepper

1 (8-ounce) package Trader Joe's Steamed and Peeled Baby Beets

Yield: 2 servings
Prep Time: 10 minutes
Cook Time: none

1. To make the gremolata, in a medium bowl, combine the lemon zest, garlic, mint, lemon juice, and olive oil. Season to taste with salt and pepper.

2. On a plate, use a butter knife to carefully cut the beets into bite-size pieces. Add the beets to the bowl with the gremolata, stirring to combine.

SUGAR SNAP PEAS with BOK CHOY

Trader Joe's island-inspired spin on teriyaki sauce gives the baby bok choy and sugar snap peas a bright, sweet boost.

1 (3-ounce) package baby bok choy

1 (12-ounce) package sugar snap peas

1 teaspoon canola oil

2 tablespoons Trader Joe's Island Soyaki

kosher salt and freshly ground black pepper

Yield: 2 servings
Prep Time: 5 minutes
Cook Time: 10 minutes

1. Cut off the stems of the baby bok choy. Cut the bok choy into pieces, making the leaves larger and the stems smaller so it all cooks evenly.

2. Microwave the sugar snap peas in their bag on high for 2 minutes.

3. Meanwhile, heat the oil in a medium skillet over medium-high heat until shimmering. Add the baby bok choy to the pan and cook, stirring constantly, until the leaves are just wilted, about 1 minute. Add the Soyaki sauce to the pan, stirring constantly. Add the peas, sautéing and stirring to coat.

4. Test a bok choy stem for tenderness and remove the pan from the heat. Season to taste with salt and pepper.

BROCCOLI with DRIED CHERRIES

This vegan side is great with a vegetarian main dish or seafood, and it can also be paired with a fattier beef dish if you're looking to balance out the meal.

kosher salt and freshly ground black pepper

2 heads broccoli

¼ cup olive oil

1 tablespoon Trader Joe's Crushed Garlic

½ teaspoon red chile pepper flakes

2 tablespoons lemon juice

½ cup dried cherries

Yield: 2 servings
Prep Time: 10 minutes
Cook Time: 10 minutes

1. Bring a medium pot three-quarters full of salted water to a boil over high heat.

2. Cut the broccoli into even bite-size pieces. When the water is boiling, add the broccoli and cook until fork-tender, about 5 minutes. Drain into a colander and reserve.

3. In the pot, heat the oil over medium-high heat until shimmering. Add the garlic and chile pepper flakes and cook, stirring constantly, for 1 minute. Remove from the heat and add the lemon juice and dried cherries. Add the cooked broccoli, stirring to combine. Season to taste with salt and pepper.

MEXICAN CORN on the COB

This is practically the only way I eat my corn on the cob these days.

1 (4-pack) Trader Joe's Corn on the Cob

2 tablespoons mayonnaise

1 tablespoon Trader Joe's Taco Seasoning Mix

1 tablespoon Trader Joe's Grated Parmigiano-Reggiano cheese

Yield: 4 pieces corn on the cob
Prep Time: 5 minutes
Cook Time: 5 minutes

1. If your pot is narrower than your ears of corn, cut them in half. Bring a medium pot three-quarters full of salted water to a boil over high heat. Add the corn, covering it with water. Cook until the kernels are bright yellow and tender, 3 to 4 minutes. Transfer the corn to a plate.

2. Using a butter knife, slather the corn with mayonnaise. Sprinkle with taco seasoning and cheese.

STUFFED PEAR HALVES

Sometimes I serve these pears on a bed of arugula for an easy, delicious salad.

1 (25-ounce) jar Trader Joe's Pear Halves in White Grape Juice (5 pear halves)

1 tablespoon cream cheese, softened in the microwave for 10 seconds

2 tablespoons Trader Joe's Crumbled Blue Cheese

6 Trader Joe's Triple Ginger Snaps

Yield: 2 servings
Prep Time: 10 minutes
Cook Time: 15 minutes

1. Preheat the oven to 400°F. Line a rimmed baking sheet with foil.

2. Arrange the pear halves on the prepared baking sheet.

3. In a small bowl, mix the cream cheese and blue cheese together. Mound a dollop of the mixture into each pear half.

4. Seal the ginger snaps into a plastic bag and pound into crumbs with a rolling pin or the bottom of a pan. Pour the crumbs over the pears. Bake until warm, about 15 minutes.

PESTO-ROASTED POTATOES

Pesto adds a flair of flavor to these roasted potatoes without much extra work.

1 (16-ounce) bag fingerling potatoes

1 tablespoon plus 2 teaspoons olive oil, divided

½ teaspoon kosher salt

¼ teaspoon freshly ground black pepper

2 tablespoons Trader Giotto's Genova Pesto

Yield: 2 servings
Prep Time: 5 minutes
Cook Time: 65 minutes

1. Preheat the oven to 400°F. Line a rimmed baking sheet with foil.

2. Cut each potato in half lengthwise. Spread the potatoes on the prepared baking sheet. Drizzle with 1 tablespoon of oil and sprinkle with the salt and pepper. Toss the potatoes to coat and arrange in a single layer. Bake until fork-tender, about 1 hour, stirring once halfway through.

3. In a small bowl, place the pesto and thin it with the remaining 2 teaspoons of oil.

4. Remove the potatoes from the oven. Drizzle the pesto sauce over the potatoes, stirring with a spatula. Return the potatoes to the oven for 5 minutes.

BAKED SWEET POTATO SPEARS with MEXICAN SPICES

These presliced sweet potato spears are a great item—no washing or slicing required.

2 (12-ounce) bags Trader Joe's Sweet Potato Spears

1½ tablespoons olive oil

1 tablespoon Trader Joe's Taco Seasoning Mix

½ teaspoon kosher salt

Yield: 2 servings
Prep Time: 5 minutes
Cook Time: 30 to 40 minutes

1. Preheat the oven to 400°F. Line a rimmed baking sheet with foil.

2. Spread the sweet potato spears on the prepared baking sheet. Drizzle with the oil and sprinkle with the taco seasoning and salt. Toss the sweet potato spears to coat and arrange in a single layer.

3. Bake until tender, 30 to 40 minutes, stirring once halfway through.

GREEN CHILE CORNBREAD MUFFINS

Enjoy these vegan muffins with a hearty dinner entrée, and then snack on a leftover muffin on the way to class.

1 egg
½ cup canola oil
¾ cup milk
1 (15-ounce) box Trader Joe's Cornbread Mix
¾ cup frozen Trader Joe's Roasted Corn, thawed
1 (4-ounce) can Trader Joe's Fire Roasted Diced Green Chiles
unsalted butter

Yield: 12 muffins
Prep Time: 10 minutes
Cook Time: 25 minutes

1. Preheat the oven to 350°F. Spray 12 muffin cups with cooking spray.

2. In a large bowl, whisk together the egg, oil, and milk. Stir in the cornbread mix, using a spoon or spatula to combine. Stir in the corn and chiles.

3. Fill each prepared muffin cup three-quarters full with batter.

4. Bake until a toothpick or knife inserted in the center of a muffin comes out clean, 20 to 25 minutes. Remove the muffins from the oven and let cool 15 to 20 minutes. Serve with butter.

Note: If you don't have a muffin tin, just bake the cornbread in an 8 x 8 x 2-inch pan and increase the baking time to 35 to 40 minutes.

GLAZED CARROTS

Roasting gives root vegetables like carrots a nice sweetness; honey enhances it even more.

1 (16-ounce) bag Trader Joe's Organics Cut and Peeled Carrots

1 tablespoon olive oil

kosher salt and freshly ground black pepper

½ orange

1 tablespoon honey

Yield: 2 servings
Prep Time: 10 minutes
Cook Time: 35 minutes

1. Preheat the oven to 400°F. Line a rimmed baking sheet with foil.

2. Spread the carrots on the prepared baking sheet. Drizzle with the oil and sprinkle with salt and pepper. Squeeze the orange half over the carrots. Toss the carrots to coat, then arrange in a single layer.

3. Bake until the carrots are fork-tender, about 30 minutes, stirring halfway through. Remove from the oven and increase the temperature to 425°F. Drizzle the honey over the carrots and return them to the oven to let the honey caramelize, about 5 minutes.

RICE and VERMICELLI

Browning and cooking the vermicelli noodles adds a nuttiness to the dish.

1 tablespoon canola oil

⅓ cup broken pieces Trader Joe's Vermicelli or Trader Joe's Angel Hair Pasta, uncooked

½ cup long-grain white rice

1 cup chicken broth, or 1 cup water and 1 (9.6-gram) pouch Trader Joe's Savory Chicken Flavor

1 tablespoon unsalted butter

kosher salt and freshly ground black pepper

Yield: 2 servings
Prep Time: 5 minutes
Cook Time: 25 minutes

1. In a medium pot, heat the oil over medium-high heat until shimmering. Add the noodles, stirring to coat. Cook, stirring constantly, until the noodles have browned, then add the rice and chicken broth.

2. Let the liquid come to a boil, then reduce the heat to low. Cover and let simmer until the rice is tender, about 20 minutes. Remove from the heat and let sit for 10 minutes.

3. Add the butter to the rice and stir. Season to taste with salt and pepper.

CURRIED COUSCOUS with APPLES

The crunch of apple and spice of curry make this dish shine.

1 tablespoon unsalted butter

¾ cup Trader Joe's Israeli Couscous

2 teaspoons curry powder

1 red apple, cut into bite-size pieces

1 cup water or chicken broth

kosher salt and freshly ground black pepper

Yield: 2 servings
Prep Time: 5 minutes
Cook Time: 12 minutes

1. In a small pot over medium-high heat, place the butter, couscous, and curry powder, stirring to coat the couscous with the butter and curry powder. Add the apple and water or chicken broth, stirring to combine. Bring the liquid to a boil, then cover the pot. Reduce the heat to low and cook until the couscous is tender, 10 to 12 minutes.

2. Remove from the heat and season with salt and pepper.

CHAPTER 10

QUICK & HEARTY BRAIN FOOD FOR FINALS

When you're struggling to cram for finals—not to mention finish that ten-page paper that's due tomorrow—you need every bit of brain power you can get to help focus your thoughts. And guess what? Nature has filled certain foods with nutrients and vitamins that work to help you concentrate throughout the day. From nuts to lentils to berries, some ingredients have been proven to strengthen mental power. Use these recipes to feed both your stomach and your mind during a hectic week of tests.

TROPICAL SMOOTHIE

Smoothies are a quick and sustaining way to get food into your system during a chaotic week.

1 cup low-fat plain yogurt
½ cup orange juice
1½ cups frozen mango chunks
1 teaspoon honey (optional)

Yield: 2 servings
Prep Time: 5 minutes
Cook Time: none

1. In a blender, place the yogurt, orange juice, mango chunks, and honey, if using.

2. Purée until the mango chunks disappear and the smoothie is thoroughly blended, 30 seconds to 1 minute.

VERY BERRY SMOOTHIE

When you're stressed and need to focus on cramming for tomorrow's test, berries are essential for your diet because scientists have determined that they lead to a clearer mind.

1½ cups Trader Joe's Lowfat Kefir Strawberry Cultured Milk
1 banana, coarsely chopped
½ (16-ounce) bag frozen Trader Joe's Very Cherry Berry Blend

Yield: 2 servings
Prep Time: 5 minutes
Cook Time: none

1. In a blender, place the cultured milk, banana, and berries.

2. Purée until the smoothie is thoroughly blended, 30 seconds to 1 minute.

OATMEAL with BERRIES and ALMONDS

The vitamins and nutrients in Trader Joe's Oatmeal Complete, combined with the brain-boosting ability of blueberries and the staying power of almonds, make this a rockin' meal to start a test day on the right foot.

2 (40-gram) packets Trader Joe's Oatmeal Complete

1¼ cups water

¼ cup frozen blueberries

½ cup milk

¼ cup sliced almonds

Yield: 1 to 2 servings
Prep Time: 1 minute
Cook Time: 3 minutes

1. Empty the oatmeal packets into a medium microwave-safe bowl. Stir in the water and frozen blueberries.

2. Microwave on high until hot, 2 to 3 minutes, stirring once halfway through.

3. Stir in the milk and top with the almonds.

MICROWAVE SCRAMBLED EGGS with SMOKED SALMON

Eggs are one of the most cost-effective ways of getting a large dose of protein into your diet, which can provide a boost of energy throughout the day.

3 large eggs

¼ teaspoon kosher salt

¼ teaspoon freshly ground black pepper

1 tablespoon water

1 tablespoon cream cheese

½ (4-ounce) package Trader Joe's Wild Smoked Sockeye Salmon, coarsely chopped

chopped chives, for garnish

Yield: 2 servings
Prep Time: 5 minutes
Cook Time: 2 to 3 minutes

1. In a medium microwave-safe dish, crack the eggs and add the salt, pepper, and water. Lightly beat the eggs with a whisk or fork to combine.

2. Microwave the eggs on high for 30 seconds. Using a spoon, combine the cooked eggs on the edge of the dish with the uncooked eggs in the middle. Microwave for 30 seconds longer. Stir again.

3. Repeat Step 2 until the scrambled eggs are fluffy and cooked, being careful not to overcook them. The total cooking time will depend on the power strength of the microwave but should be 2 to 3 minutes.

4. Remove the scrambled eggs from the microwave and stir in the cream cheese and smoked salmon. Top with the chives.

TRAIL MIX with CHOCOLATE-COVERED EDAMAME

It's the caffeine and sugar from dark chocolate that can give you a slight boost of energy to improve brain power.

1 cup Trader Joe's Roasted and Salted Mixed Nuts

1 cup Trader Joe's Dark Chocolate Edamame

1 (1.2-ounce) package Trader Joe's Freeze Dried Strawberries or Trader Joe's Freeze Dried Mango

Yield: 2 servings
Prep Time: 5 minutes
Cook Time: none

1. In a small bowl, combine the nuts, edamame, and fruit.

2. Transfer the trail mix to a sealable plastic bag for easier portability.

POTATO FRITTATA

A frittata is akin to an omelet, except the ingredients are mixed with the eggs instead of folded inside of them—and it's a heck of a lot easier to make.

4 hashbrowns from frozen Trader Joe's Hashbrowns

1 tablespoon canola oil

3 large eggs

½ teaspoon kosher salt

¼ teaspoon freshly ground black pepper

½ cup Trader Joe's Shredded Pepper Jack Cheese Blend

Yield: 2 to 3 servings
Prep Time: 5 minutes
Cook Time: 10 minutes

1. Preheat the oven to 400°F.

2. Toast the hash browns in a toaster to defrost. Chop the hash browns into medium dice.

3. In an oven-safe nonstick skillet, heat the oil over medium-high heat until shimmering. Add the hash browns in a single layer, frying until slightly crisp on each side, 6 to 7 minutes total.

4. Meanwhile, in a medium bowl, place the eggs, salt, and pepper. Mix together with a fork or a whisk.

5. Pour the eggs on top of the hash browns, gently stirring with a spatula until the egg mixture has set on the bottom, 1 to 2 minutes.

6. Transfer the pan to the oven and bake until the top of the frittata is almost set and puffy. Sprinkle with the cheese and continue to bake until the cheese melts, 1 to 2 minutes more.

SALMON BURGERS with TZATZIKI

Salmon is rich in DHA, an omega-3 fatty acid that's full of brain-boosting power, which improves your attention span in times of marathon studying or test taking.

2 teaspoons canola oil

2 Trader Joe's Premium Salmon Burgers

2 Trader Joe's Honey Wheat Hamburger Buns

2 tablespoons Trader Joe's Tzatziki (creamy garlic cucumber dip)

Yield: 2 sandwiches
Prep Time: 1 minute
Cook Time: 8 minutes

1. In a nonstick skillet, heat the oil over medium-high heat until shimmering.

2. Add the salmon patties and cook until done, 3 to 4 minutes per side. Pierce one of the patties with a small knife to see whether it's cooked to your liking.

3. Meanwhile, warm the buns in the microwave for 15 to 30 seconds.

4. Place the salmon patties on the hamburger bun bottoms. Top generously with the tzatziki and add the bun tops.

WARMED CHICKEN SALAD with GREEN TEA

Edamame is a powerful protein source to help you get through a mammoth week of work, and green tea is a rock star for the brain.

1 (12-ounce) package Trader Joe's Just Chicken White Meat

½ cup Trader Joe's Shelled Edamame

1 tablespoon mayonnaise

¼ teaspoon kosher salt

¼ teaspoon freshly ground black pepper

1 scallion, chopped

1 tea bag Trader Joe's Green Tea

Yield: 2 servings
Prep Time: 5 minutes
Cook Time: 5 minutes

1. Heat the chicken breast according to the package directions, then cut the chicken into bite-size pieces.

2. In a medium bowl, place the soybeans, mayonnaise, salt, pepper, and scallion. Open the tea bag, measure 1 teaspoon green tea leaves, and add it to the mixture. Discard the remainder of the tea bag.

3. Stir the mayonnaise mixture together, then add the chicken chunks and stir to combine.

HARVEST GRAINS BLEND with SPINACH

Greens, like spinach, are a superstar source of folate and vitamin B, which lead to better memory recall. Trader Joe's Harvest Grains Blend is a hearty, tasty mix of Israeli couscous, baby chickpeas, orzo, and red quinoa that will keep you full and focused during a cram session.

1 tablespoon olive oil

1 (6-ounce) bag baby spinach

1¼ cups Trader Joe's Harvest Grains Blend

1¾ cups vegetable or chicken broth

½ teaspoon kosher salt, or more to taste

¼ teaspoon freshly ground black pepper, or more to taste

Yield: 2 servings
Prep Time: 5 minutes
Cook Time: 15 minutes

1. In a medium pot, heat the oil over medium-high heat until shimmering.

2. Add half the spinach, stirring until wilted, about 1 minute. Add the remaining spinach, stirring until wilted, about 1 minute longer.

3. Add the grains, stirring to coat with the oil. Pour in the vegetable or chicken broth, stirring to combine with the grains. Add the salt and pepper, stir, and bring to a boil.

4. Reduce the heat to low. Cover the pot and let simmer until all of the liquid has been absorbed, 12 to 15 minutes. Taste and adjust the seasonings with salt and pepper, as needed.

The I ♥ TRADER JOE'S® COLLEGE COOKBOOK

ROASTED CHICKEN with LEEKS and APPLES

Apples are known to improve cognitive function—as if you need an excuse to add more apples to your diet.

1 tablespoon canola oil

4 pieces Trader Joe's Organic Free Range Chicken Boneless Thighs

½ teaspoon kosher salt, or more to taste

¼ teaspoon freshly ground black pepper, or more to taste

1 (6-ounce) package Trader Joe's Trimmed Leeks, cut in half lengthwise, then crosswise into 1-inch pieces

½ (16-ounce) bag Trader Joe's Sliced Apples

1 tablespoon unsalted butter, cut into small pieces

Yield: 2 servings
Prep Time: 10 minutes
Cook Time: 35 minutes

1. Preheat the oven to 400°F.

2. In a medium oven-safe skillet, heat the oil over medium-high heat until shimmering.

3. Season the chicken thighs with salt and pepper. Add the chicken to the oil and cook just 2 to 3 minutes, letting the bottom sides of the chicken brown.

4. Remove the chicken from the skillet. Add the leeks and apples to the skillet and place the chicken pieces on top. Scatter the butter over and transfer the skillet to the oven. Bake for 30 minutes, stirring once halfway through. Cut into the thickest chicken piece to determine that it's no longer pink. Adjust the seasoning with salt and pepper, as needed.

LENTIL SOUP with CHICKEN SAUSAGE

Lentils significantly reduce blood glucose levels, which powers the body with sustained energy throughout the day.

1 (17-ounce) box Trader Joe's Organic Lentil Vegetable Soup

½ cup water or chicken broth

½ (14-ounce) package Trader Joe's Smoked Andouille Chicken Sausage

juice of ½ lime

¼ cup chopped cilantro (optional)

Yield: 2 servings
Prep Time: 5 minutes
Cook Time: 10 minutes

1. To a medium pot, add the lentil soup and water or broth. Bring to a boil over high heat.

2. Meanwhile, cut the sausage into bite-size pieces. When the soup is boiling, stir in the sausage. Reduce the heat to medium and simmer for 5 minutes to let the sausage warm. Stir in the lime juice and serve immediately with the cilantro, if using.

CHAPTER 11

SPECIAL OCCASIONS

Let's face facts: You're busy in college and don't want to devote a ton of time to cooking. That's why most of the recipes in this book lean toward the quick and easy side of things.

But sometimes, just sometimes, you want to cook a little something special. Maybe you've worked hard all week through a slew of tests and deserve a special Saturday dinner. Or you're hosting your first dinner party, having a romantic date, or just want something a little fancy.

These recipes deliver on your occasional need to take dinner to the next level. Don't worry—they're still on the easy side. But they'll taste like you've been slaving for hours.

EGGPLANT PARMESAN LASAGNA

Take a few Trader Joe's ingredients, mix them together, and voilà—you have an impressive dinner either to serve when guests come over or to take to a potluck.

1 (15-ounce) container Trader Giotto's Traditional Fresh Ricotta

1 large egg

1 cup Trader Joe's Grated Parmigiano-Reggiano cheese, plus more to top (optional)

1 (16-ounce) bag frozen Trader Giotto's Misto alla Griglia

1 (25-ounce) jar Trader Giotto's Organic Tomato Basil Marinara

8 Trader Joe's No Boil Italian Lasagna Noodles

Yield: 4 servings
Prep Time: 15 minutes
Cook Time: 65 minutes

1. Preheat the oven to 375°F.

2. In a medium bowl, stir together the ricotta, egg, and Parmigiano-Reggiano, if using.

3. In a small baking dish, start assembling the lasagna: Arrange 4 to 5 eggplant pieces in the bottom. Top with one-third of the tomato sauce and 2 lasagna noodles.

4. Next, layer one-half of the ricotta mixture and 2 more lasagna noodles on top. Arrange a second layer of 4 to 5 eggplant pieces in the dish, then one-third of the tomato sauce and 2 more lasagna noodles.

5. Add the remaining one-half of the ricotta mixture and top with the remaining 2 lasagna noodles.

6. Pour the remaining one-third of the tomato sauce over the lasagna. Cover the dish with foil. Bake until the noodles are fully cooked, 60 to 65 minutes. Remove from the oven and top with extra Parmigiano-Reggiano cheese, if desired.

The I ♥ TRADER JOE'S® COLLEGE COOKBOOK

SALMON with MIREPOIX

This is based on a Julia Child recipe in which salmon is cooked on a bed of onion, celery, and carrots with white wine.

1 tablespoon canola oil

1 (14.5-ounce) container Trader Joe's Mirepoix (onion, celery, and carrots)

3 tablespoons carrot juice

1 frozen Trader Joe's Wild Alaskan Sockeye Salmon Fillet (about 1 pound), thawed

½ teaspoon kosher salt

¼ teaspoon freshly ground black pepper

juice of ½ lemon

Yield: 4 servings
Prep Time: 10 minutes
Cook Time: 20 minutes

1. Preheat the oven to 350°F.

2. In a large oven-safe skillet, heat the oil over medium-high heat until shimmering.

3. Add the mirepoix to the pan and cook, stirring occasionally, until the onion is soft, about 5 minutes. Remove the skillet from the heat. Add the carrot juice and stir to combine.

4. Season the salmon with salt and pepper, and place it on top of the vegetable mixture. Cover the pan with foil.

5. Bake for 12 to 15 minutes, depending on the size and thickness of the salmon fillet. Pierce the salmon with a small knife to see whether it's cooked to your liking. Remove from the oven and drizzle with lemon juice.

CRAB CAKES BENEDICT

This is a fancy brunch meal for when the occasion arises.

4 teaspoons olive oil, divided

1 (6-ounce) bag baby spinach

1 teaspoon Trader Joe's Crushed Garlic

2 (6-ounce) packages Trader Joe's Maryland Style Crab Cakes

2 whole grain English muffins

2 to 3 tablespoons Trader Joe's Hollandaise Sauce

chopped chives, for garnish

Yield: 4 servings
Prep Time: 5 minutes
Cook Time: 10 minutes

1. In a nonstick skillet, heat 2 teaspoons of oil over high heat until shimmering. Add one-half of the spinach, stirring until wilted, about 1 minute. Add the garlic and the remaining spinach, stirring until all the spinach is wilted and the garlic is golden, about 1 minute longer. Transfer the spinach to a bowl and set aside.

2. Wipe the pan clean with a paper towel. Heat the remaining 2 teaspoons of oil over medium-high heat until shimmering. Add the frozen crab cakes to the pan and cook until hot, about 2 minutes per side. Split the muffins and toast.

3. Place a muffin half on each plate. Pile each one with one-fourth of the reserved spinach and top with a crab cake.

4. In a microwave-safe dish, microwave the hollandaise sauce on high until warm, about 1 minute. Drizzle the sauce over the crab cakes and garnish with the chives.

SPAGHETTI in CREAMY TOMATO SAUCE with LANGOUSTINES

This is the dish to make for a special occasion, Trader Joe's–style.

¾ (16-ounce) package Trader Giotto's Organic Spaghetti

1 tablespoon olive oil

½ (20-ounce) package Trader Joe's Tomato Feta Soup

¼ teaspoon kosher salt

¼ teaspoon freshly ground black pepper

1 (12-ounce) bag frozen Trader Joe's Langoustine Tails, thawed and drained

¼ cup Trader Joe's Crumbled Feta (optional)

Yield: 4 servings
Prep Time: 5 minutes
Cook Time: 15 minutes

1. Cook the spaghetti according to the package directions. Reserve ½ cup of the pasta water, and then drain the pasta and toss with the oil.

2. To a large skillet, add the tomato soup and reserved pasta water, and heat over medium, 4 to 5 minutes. Season with salt and pepper.

3. Add the langoustines to the pan and cook until just warm, 1 to 2 minutes. (The langoustines are already fully cooked, so be careful not to overcook them.)

4. Remove from the heat and stir in the pasta, using tongs. Top with the feta cheese, if using.

Note: Langoustines are small, pink crustaceans that look similar to crawfish with a taste more akin to lobster.

LEMON PASTA with ALFREDO SAUCE and SEAFOOD

This is a luxurious, indulgent pasta that will impress any guest.

2 (8-ounce) packages Trader Joe's Lemon Pepper Pappardelle Pasta

2 tablespoons olive oil

1 (16-ounce) package frozen Trader Joe's Seafood Blend

1 (16.9-ounce) jar Trader Giotto's Alfredo Pasta Sauce or 1 (15-ounce) jar Trader Joe's Limone Alfredo Sauce

2 tablespoons chopped chives, for garnish

Yield: 4 servings
Prep Time: 10 minutes
Cook Time: 14 minutes

1. Bring a medium pot of salted water to a boil over high heat. Cook the pappardelle until al dente (see page 193), about 8 minutes.

2. Meanwhile, add the oil to a large skillet and heat on medium-high. To the skillet, add the seafood blend and cook for 2 to 3 minutes, until the seafood is cooked. Add the Alfredo sauce or limone Alfredo sauce. Cook for 2 to 3 minutes until the sauce is warm. Remove from the heat.

3. Add the cooked pasta to the sauce and toss to coat. Garnish with the chives and serve immediately.

ISRAELI COUSCOUS with LEMON SHRIMP

When you're short on time but need to whip up an impressive dish for a date, this is the one to turn to.

2½ tablespoons unsalted butter, divided

1½ cups Israeli couscous

2 cups water

kosher salt and freshly ground black pepper

juice of 2 lemons

½ cup olive oil

½ cup Trader Joe's Grated Parmigiano-Reggiano cheese

1 (16-ounce) bag frozen Trader Joe's Uncooked Wild Blue Shrimp, thawed

Yield: 4 servings
Prep Time: 5 minutes
Cook Time: 12 minutes

1. In a medium pot over medium-high heat, melt 1 tablespoon of butter. Add the couscous, stirring to coat with butter.

2. Add the water to the couscous and season with salt and pepper. Bring the liquid to a boil, then cover the pot. Reduce the heat to low and cook until the couscous is tender, 10 to 12 minutes.

3. Meanwhile, in a small bowl, combine the lemon juice, oil, and cheese.

4. In a medium skillet over high heat, melt the remaining 1½ tablespoons of butter. Add the shrimp and sauté until cooked and pink, 2 to 3 minutes. Remove from the heat and add the lemon sauce. Pour the shrimp and lemon sauce over the couscous, stirring to combine.

RAVIOLI with BROWN BUTTER SAUCE

Brown butter is a rich, nutty sauce that's easy to prepare and makes you look like an ace in the kitchen.

2 (8.8-ounce) packages Trader Joe's Cacio E Pepe Ravioli

5 tablespoons unsalted butter

⅓ (7-ounce) bag arugula

Yield: 4 servings
Prep Time: none
Cook Time: 10 minutes

1. Bring a medium pot of salted water to a boil over high heat. Cook the ravioli until al dente (see page 193), 4 to 6 minutes. Drain the pasta in a colander and set aside.

2. In a large saucepan over high heat, melt the butter, stirring constantly. Cook the butter until it gets frothy and turns a golden color, about 2 minutes. Remove from the heat.

3. Add the arugula, stirring until it wilts. Stir in the ravioli, coating it in the brown butter and arugula.

CHICKEN with 40 CLOVES of GARLIC

This is one of my favorite recipes, and not just because it tastes like it took hours to prepare. Serve with crusty French bread to spread the soft garlic on.

1 tablespoon canola oil

1 package Trader Joe's Organic Free Range Chicken Boneless Thighs (about 1½ pounds)

½ teaspoon kosher salt

¼ teaspoon freshly ground black pepper

1 cup chicken broth or hot water

1 (4-ounce) bag Trader Joe's Premium Peeled Garlic

4 to 6 sprigs fresh thyme

Yield: 4 servings
Prep Time: 5 minutes
Cook Time: 40 minutes

1. Preheat the oven to 375°F.

2. In a large oven-safe pot, heat the oil over medium-high heat until shimmering.

3. Season the chicken thighs with salt and pepper and add them to the pot. Sear briefly on each side until slightly golden in color, about 2 minutes per side.

4. Add the chicken broth, garlic, and thyme to the pot, stirring to combine. Remove from the heat and cover the pot.

5. Bake in the oven until the chicken thighs are done, 30 to 35 minutes. Cut into the thickest chicken piece to determine that it's no longer pink. Remove the thyme sprigs and serve the chicken with the garlic cloves and broth drizzled over the top.

BAKED FETA and TOMATO PASTA

The ingredients for this dish are a little more pricey than others in this book. But this viral pasta dish is easy and awe-inspiring when entertaining guests.

1 (16-ounce) container Trader Joe's Mini Heirloom Tomatoes

1 (10.5-ounce) container Trader Joe's Authentic Greek Feta in Brine

¼ teaspoon kosher salt

¼ teaspoon freshly ground black pepper

¼ cup olive oil

4 to 6 cloves garlic, peeled

¾ (16-ounce) package Trader Joe's Organic Penne Rigate

Yield: 4 servings
Prep Time: 5 minutes
Cook Time: 50 minutes

1. Preheat the oven to 400°F. Add the tomatoes to a 9 x 13-inch baking dish. Drain the brine from the feta cheese and add the cheese to the center of the baking dish. Season with salt and pepper. Drizzle the oil over the mixture and add the garlic cloves.

2. Bake until the cheese is fully melted and the tomatoes are soft, 30 to 40 minutes.

3. Meanwhile, cook the pasta according to the package directions. Drain in a colander.

4. Carefully remove the baking dish from the oven and add the cooked pasta to the baking dish. Toss to combine. Serve immediately.

WASABI-COATED CHICKEN

Pour a beer on the side and these greenish chicken tenders are fine fare for a St. Paddy's Day celebration.

1½ cups Trader Joe-San Wasabi Peas

1 cup Trader Joe's Japanese-Style Panko Bread Crumbs

1 cup whole milk

1 large egg

kosher salt and freshly ground black pepper

1 pound Trader Joe's Organic Free Range Chicken Breast Tenders

kosher salt and freshly ground black pepper

canola oil, as needed

Yield: 3 to 4 servings
Prep Time: 15 minutes
Cook Time: 20 minutes

1. Preheat the oven to 350°F.

2. Seal the wasabi peas into a plastic bag and pound them into crumbs. If you have a blender, you can also use that to crumble the peas. Place the crumbs in a medium bowl and mix in the panko bread crumbs.

3. In another medium bowl, use a fork or whisk to beat the milk and egg together to combine.

4. Season both sides of the chicken with salt and pepper. Dip each chicken tender into the milk-egg mixture and then into the wasabi-panko mixture.

5. In a medium skillet, heat 1 inch of oil over medium-high heat until shimmering. Add several chicken tenders (do not crowd the pan) and cook until the crust turns golden, about 1 minute per side. Remove the fried tenders to a rimmed baking sheet. Repeat until all the chicken tenders have been fried.

6. Transfer the baking sheet to the oven and bake until the chicken tenders are fully cooked, 6 to 8 minutes. Cut into the thickest chicken tender to determine it's no longer pink.

7. Remove from the oven and sprinkle with salt.

CHAPTER 12

AIR FRYER

For any avid shopper of Trader Joe's, an air fryer is a must-have. Trader Joe's frozen foods excel in the air fryer—they become crispy as can be without any added oil (just a spritz of cooking spray will do) in the fraction of the time that it would cook in the oven. So if you haven't yet splurged on an air fryer, consider adding it to a birthday or holiday wish list. For those who already have one, get ready for the best chicken wings you've ever made at home, with a General Tsao's spin. Trader Joe's toasted ravioli are oozy, cheesy magic and get transformed into nachos, thanks to five-layer dip. Breaded chicken tenders turn into an easy air fryer chicken parmesan. So what are you waiting for?

GENERAL TSAO'S AIR-FRIED WINGS

Who needs a deep fryer when an air fryer renders chicken wings that are perfectly crispy? A toss in General Tsao Stir Fry Sauce gives these wings a unique touch.

Trader Joe's All Natural Fresh Chicken Wings (around 2 pounds)

1 tablespoon olive oil

½ teaspoon kosher salt

1 teaspoon baking powder (optional)

2 tablespoons butter, melted

¼ cup Trader Ming's General Tsao Stir Fry Sauce

1 tablespoon Trader Joe's Sriracha Sauce

sesame seeds, as needed (optional)

2 scallions, chopped (optional)

Yield: 4 servings
Prep Time: 5 minutes
Cook Time: 50 minutes

1. In a large bowl or ziplock bag, toss the frozen chicken wing sections with the oil, salt, and baking powder, if using. Add half of the chicken wings to the air fryer in one layer. Bake the chicken wings at 380°F for 15 minutes, shaking the basket as needed.

2. Using tongs, flip the chicken wings over. Increase the air fryer temperature to 400°F. Continue to cook the chicken wings for 10 more minutes, until fully cooked, shaking the basket as needed.

3. To a large bowl, add the butter, stir fry sauce, and sriracha. Add the cooked chicken wings, tossing with the sauce. Using tongs, transfer the wings from the sauce to a plate. Repeat with the remaining chicken and sauce, heating the sauce slightly in the microwave before tossing with the wings. Sprinkle with the sesame seeds and scallions, if using. Serve immediately.

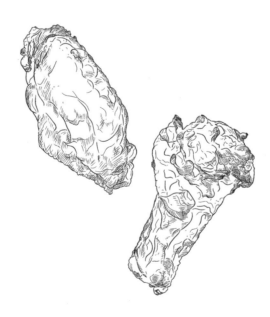

EXTRA-SPICY ITALIAN AIR-FRIED WINGS

These spicy wings, taken straight from the freezer, can be whipped up in no time. The Italian Bomba Hot Pepper Sauce packs quite the punch, so use it cautiously.

½ (32-ounce) package frozen Trader Joe's Organic Chicken Wing Sections

1 tablespoon olive oil

½ teaspoon kosher salt

1 teaspoon baking powder (optional)

2 tablespoon butter, melted

¼ cup Trader Joe's Italian Bomba Hot Pepper Sauce

Yield: 2 servings
Prep Time: 5 minutes
Cook Time: 30 minutes

1. In a large bowl or a ziplock bag, toss the frozen chicken wing sections with oil, salt, and baking powder, if using. Add to the air fryer in one layer. Bake the chicken wings at 370°F for 15 minutes, shaking the basket as needed.

2. Increase the air fryer temperature to 400°F. Continue to cook the chicken wings for 10 to 15 more minutes, until fully cooked, shaking the basket as needed.

3. To a large bowl, add the butter and hot pepper sauce. Add the chicken wings, tossing with the sauce. Serve immediately.

AIR FRYER TOASTED RAVIOLI NACHOS

Make a meal out of these breaded ravioli by turning them into nachos, as in this recipe, or by dipping them in marinara sauce.

½ (16-ounce) bag Trader Joe's Breaded Fried Ravioli

½ (21-ounce) container Trader Joe's Five Layer Dip

Yield: 2 servings
Prep Time: 5 minutes
Cook Time: 10 minutes

1. Spray the air fryer basket with cooking spray. Add the fried ravioli to the basket in an even layer. Spray the ravioli tops with cooking spray. Cook at 390°F for 6 minutes. Flip the ravioli and spray the tops again with cooking spray. Cook for another 2 to 4 minutes, until some of the ravioli have puffed up.

2. Transfer the fried ravioli to a plate and top with dollops of the dip. Serve immediately.

AIR FRYER FISH AND CHIPS

If you don't have the condiments on hand to make the homemade tartar sauce, feel free to use Trader Joe's Tartar Sauce.

2 Trader Joe's Breaded Tilapia Fillets

1½ cups Trader Joe's Handsome Cut Potato Fries

¼ cup mayonnaise

2 teaspoons lemon juice

1 tablespoon Trader Joe's Sweet Organic Relish

1 teaspoon capers, roughly chopped

⅛ teaspoon kosher salt

⅛ teaspoon freshly ground black pepper

Yield: 2 servings
Prep Time: 5 minutes
Cook Time: 12 minutes

1. Spray the air fryer basket with cooking spray. Add the breaded tilapia and fries to the basket in an even layer. Spray the tilapia and fries with cooking spray. Cook at 390°F for 8 minutes. Flip the fish and fries; bake for another 2 to 4 minutes until done. If the fries are getting too crispy, remove with tongs and let the fish finish cooking.

2. Meanwhile, in a small bowl, combine the mayonnaise, lemon juice, relish, and capers. Season with salt and pepper. Serve the fish and fries with the tartar sauce.

AIR FRYER PIZZA

An Indian flatbread makes the perfect pizza crust when crisped in the air fryer. Trader Joe's Toscano cheese melts like a dream.

2 pieces Trader Joe's Traditional Indian Style Flatbread

½–⅔ cup Trader Joe's Pizza Sauce, Trader Joe's Organic Vodka Pasta Sauce, or any other tomato sauce, divided

½ cup Trader Joe's Shredded Pizza Seasoned Toscano Cheese, divided

Trader Joe's Honey Aleppo Pepper Sauce (optional)

Yield: 2 servings
Prep Time: 5 minutes
Cook Time: 20 minutes

1. Place 1 flatbread in the air fryer and cook at 390°F for 3 to 5 minutes until the flatbread is crisp, checking often to make sure it doesn't burn.

2. Carefully remove the air fryer basket. Using tongs, flip the flatbread over. Spread ¼ to ⅓ cup of tomato sauce over the flatbread, and top with ¼ cup of cheese. Continue to cook at 390°F in the air fryer for another 3 to 5 minutes, until the edges are golden and the cheese is melted. Let cool slightly before cutting. Repeat with the remaining ingredients. To serve, drizzle with the pepper sauce, if using.

NASHVILLE-STYLE CHICKEN AND WAFFLES

8 to 10 Trader Joe's Breaded Chicken Tenderloin Breasts

4 Trader Joe's Belgian Waffles or Trader Joe's Multi Grain Toaster Waffles

1 tablespoon butter

¼ cup Trader Joe's Organic Maple Syrup

1 tablespoon Trader Joe's Jalapeño Pepper Hot Sauce

Yield: 2 servings
Prep Time: 5 minutes
Cook Time: 10 minutes

1. Spray the air fryer basket with cooking spray. Add the breaded chicken to the basket. Spray the chicken with cooking spray. Cook at 400°F for 5 minutes per side.

2. Meanwhile, toast the waffles in a toaster until golden and crisp. Spread the waffles lightly with butter. In a small bowl, combine the maple syrup and hot sauce.

3. Place 2 waffles on each plate. Top with the chicken pieces. Drizzle the spicy maple syrup over the top and serve immediately.

AIR FRYER CHICKEN PARMESAN

Eat these chicken Parmesan pieces on their own, or serve on rolls for a chicken Parm sandwich.

8 to 10 Trader Joe's Breaded Chicken Tenderloin Breasts

½ cup Trader Joe's Tomato-Basil Marinara or any other tomato sauce

¼ cup Trader Joe's Shredded Mozzarella or Trader Joe's Shredded Pizza Seasoned Toscano Cheese

2 tablespoons Trader Joe's Parmesan, Romano, and Asiago Blend

Yield: 2 servings
Prep Time: 5 minutes
Cook Time: 12 minutes

1. Spray the air fryer basket with cooking spray. Add the breaded chicken breasts and spray the chicken with cooking spray. Cook at 400°F for 5 minutes. Flip the chicken and spray again with the cooking spray. Cook for another 5 minutes.

2. Carefully remove the basket. Spoon the marinara or other tomato sauce over the chicken, and sprinkle with the shredded mozzarella or shredded Toscano cheese. Cook for 1 to 2 minutes, until the cheese melts. Garnish with the Parmesan. Serve immediately.

AIR FRYER BUTTERNUT SQUASH FRIES

Trader Joe's has already done the hard work of cutting butternut squash into cute zig-zag shapes, which can be turned into a crunchy side or appetizer.

1 (12-ounce) container Trader Joe's Butternut Squash Zig-Zags

½ teaspoon Trader Joe's Everything But the Elote Seasoning Blend

¼ teaspoon salt

Trader Joe's Chunky Blue Cheese Dressing or Dip or Trader Joe's Green Goddess Dressing, as needed

Yield: 4 servings
Prep Time: none
Cook Time: 30 minutes

1. In a large bowl, toss the zig-zags with the elote seasoning blend and salt. Coat the air fryer basket with cooking spray and add about half of the zig-zags in one layer to the basket. Coat the zig-zags with cooking spray.

2. Cook at 400°F for 12 to 15 minutes, until crisp, shaking occasionally. Remove and repeat with the remaining zig-zags. Serve the warm ones immediately with the blue cheese dressing or dip or the green goddess dressing.

AIR-FRIED DOUBLE-STUFFED JOE-JOE'S

No need to go to a carnival to get a fried cookie fix. With just a handful of ingredients and an air fryer, you can make these desserts anytime.

8 Joe-Joe's Chocolate Vanilla Creme Cookies

½ (8-ounce) can Trader Joe's Crescent Rolls

¼ cup confectioners' sugar

Yield: 4 servings
Prep Time: 5 minutes
Cook Time: 6 minutes

1. Remove the top layer of each chocolate vanilla creme cookie, reserving them for another use (or just eat them now). Put the 2 bottom layers together to form 4 double-stuffed Joe-Joes'.

2. Using your fingers, gently stretch the triangular dough for 1 crescent roll. Wrap the dough around 1 double-stuffed cookie, enclosing the cookie as fully in the dough as you can. Repeat with the remaining 3 double-stuffed cookies and 3 triangles of dough.

3. Coat the air fryer basket with cooking spray. Place the cookies, seam-side down, in the basket. Spray the tops with cooking spray. Cook at 380°F for 3 minutes per side. Dust with the confectioners' sugar and serve.

CHAPTER 13

INSTANT POT

Oh, how I wish Instant Pots existed when I was in college. They're the ultimate portable cooking vessel—no oven or stove needed! Armed with an Instant Pot and a handful of ingredients, you can create complete meals, like a whole chicken, for yourself and friends, chili for a Super Bowl party, or pulled pork sandwiches for a crowd. A stovetop isn't even required for Trader Joe's boxed shells and cheese. In this chapter, that ingredient is revamped into cheesy pasta with ground beef but you can also just make mac and cheese. An Instant Pot is one of my favorite ways to cook risotto since there's no slaving over a pot, stirring constantly. It's mind-blowing just how much an Instant Pot + Trader Joe's ingredients can do.

INSTANT POT SPINACH-ARTICHOKE FETTUCCINE

Trader Joe's popular Creamy Spinach & Artichoke Dip also makes an easy pasta sauce, especially when the Instant Pot does all the work.

3 cups water

12 ounces Trader Joe's Authentic Fettuccine

½ cup frozen chopped spinach

¼ teaspoon kosher salt

¼ teaspoon freshly ground black pepper

1 (8.8-ounce) package frozen Trader Joe's Creamy Spinach & Artichoke Dip

1 (8.8-ounce) can Trader Joe's Whole Artichokes

⅓ cup Trader Joe's Parmesan, Romano, and Asiago Blend, for garnish (optional)

Yield: 4 servings
Prep Time: 5 minutes
Cook Time: 8 minutes
Release Time: 17 minutes

1. To the Instant Pot, add the water, fettuccine, and frozen spinach. Make sure the fettuccine is fully submerged in the liquid. Season with the salt and pepper. Place the frozen spinach and artichoke dip on top of the mixture.

2. Seal the Instant Pot and cook on high pressure for 8 minutes. Immediately do a quick release of the steam pressure. Stir together to break apart any noodles that are stuck together. Let sit for a few minutes to thicken.

3. Meanwhile, drain the artichokes and rinse well with water. Roughly chop the artichokes and stir into the pasta. Garnish the pasta with the cheese, if using, and serve.

INSTANT POT LINGUINE with VODKA SAUCE and IMPOSSIBLE GROUND BEEF

Although this one-pot wonder uses Impossible Burger meat, regular ground meat will also work, although it will need to be sautéed for a few minutes longer.

1 tablespoon canola oil

1 (12-ounce) package Impossible Plant-Based Ground Burger Meat

3 cups water

12 ounces Trader Joe's Authentic Linguine

1 (25-ounce) Trader Joe's Organic Vodka Pasta Sauce or any other tomato sauce

¼ teaspoon kosher salt

¼ teaspoon freshly ground black pepper

⅓ cup Trader Joe's Parmesan, Romano, and Asiago Blend, for garnish (optional)

Yield: 4 servings
Prep Time: 5 minutes
Cook Time: 14 minutes
Release Time: 11 minutes

1. Using the Instant Pot's sauté function on medium, heat the oil. Add the plant-based meat. Cook for 3 to 4 minutes until mostly brown, stirring to break up. Turn off the sauté function. Add the water and, using a spatula or wooden spoon, scrape up any browned bits.

2. Break the linguine in half and add to the pot. Pour the vodka sauce or any other tomato sauce over the pasta; do not stir but make sure the linguine is fully submerged in the liquid. Season with salt and pepper; do not stir.

3. Seal the Instant Pot and cook on high pressure for 10 minutes. Immediately do a quick release of the steam pressure. Stir together and serve garnished with the cheese, if using.

INSTANT POT SPAGHETTI SQUASH
with SPICY ALFREDO SAUCE

Not only is cooking a spaghetti squash much quicker in an Instant Pot than in an oven, but you also don't risk cutting yourself while trying to halve a tricky squash. To turn this into a heartier meal, add in 2 sliced links of Trader Joe's Sweet Italian Style Chicken Sausage, which is already cooked.

1 (1½-pound) spaghetti squash

1 cup water

½ cup Trader Joe's Alfredo Pasta Sauce

2 teaspoons Trader Joe's Italian Bomba Hot Pepper Sauce

¼ teaspoon kosher salt

¼ teaspoon freshly ground black pepper

Yield: 2 servings
Prep Time: 5 minutes
Cook Time: 20 minutes
Release Time: 5 minutes

1. Pierce the spaghetti squash a few times with a knife. Add the wire rack to the Instant Pot. Add the water and place the spaghetti squash on the rack. Seal the Instant Pot and set to high pressure. Cook for 15 to 20 minutes, depending on the size of the squash, with a 1½-pound spaghetti squash needing 20 minutes. Do a quick release of the steam pressure.

2. Carefully remove the spaghetti squash from the Instant Pot. Let cool slightly. Halve lengthwise, removing the seeds. Use a fork to shred the strands.

3. Add the Alfredo sauce to a medium microwave-safe dish, and microwave for 1 to 2 minutes until warm. Stir in the hot pepper sauce, salt, and pepper. Add the spaghetti squash strands, tossing to coat. Serve.

INSTANT POT CREAMY LEMON ORZO and SHRIMP

This creamy orzo dish for two is easy-peasy, thanks to the Instant Pot.

½ cup Trader Joe's Italian Orzo

½ cup water

1 (16-ounce) package frozen Trader Joe's Jumbo Cooked & Deveined Shrimp

½ cup frozen Trader Joe's Organic Peas

½ cup Trader Joe's Limone Alfredo Sauce

¼ teaspoon kosher salt

¼ teaspoon freshly ground black pepper

Yield: 2 servings
Prep Time: 2 minutes
Cook Time: 3 minutes
Release Time: 17 minutes

1. In an Instant Pot, layer the orzo, water, shrimp, and peas. Pour the Alfredo sauce on top but do not stir. Season with the salt and pepper; do not stir.

2. Seal the Instant Pot and cook on high pressure for 3 minutes. Immediately do a quick release of the steam pressure. Stir together. Let sit for 5 minutes so that the sauce can thicken. Serve immediately.

INSTANT POT WHOLE SPATCHCOCKED CHICKEN

The Instant Pot braises the flavorful, citrus-marinated chicken so well that you'll never cook a whole chicken another way. Serve with Trader Joe's Mashed Potatoes for a complete meal for 4 with only 5 ingredients.

1 cup water

1 Trader Joe's Spatchcocked Lemon Rosemary Chicken

½ teaspoon kosher salt

¼ teaspoon freshly ground black pepper

Yield: 4 servings
Prep Time: 5 minutes
Cook Time: 23 minutes
Release Time: 20 minutes

1. Place the trivet in the Instant Pot along with the water. Add the chicken to the Instant Pot on top of the trivet, breast-side up. Season with salt and pepper.

2. Seal the Instant Pot and cook on high pressure for 23 minutes. Do a natural release of the steam pressure for at least 20 minutes. Remove the chicken from the Instant Pot, and let rest for 10 minutes before carving. Serve.

EASY INSTANT POT CHILI

For a Super Bowl feast or just a regular dinner with friends, turn to this comforting chili recipe.

½ cup water

1 tablespoon Trader Joe's Chili Seasoning Blend or chili powder

1 (15.5-ounce) can Trader Joe's Kidney Beans, drained and rinsed

1 (15.5-ounce) can Trader Joe's Organic Pinto Beans

1 (14.5-ounce) can Trader Joe's Diced & No Salt Added Organic Tomatoes

1 (12-ounce) package frozen Trader Joe's "Just Sauce" Turkey Bolognese

¼ teaspoon kosher salt

1 tablespoon Trader Joe's Italian Bomba Hot Pepper Sauce (optional)

1 (2.11-ounce) bag Trader Giotto's Oven Baked Cheese Bites or ½ cup grated cheddar cheese

Yield: 4 servings
Prep Time: 5 minutes
Cook Time: 15 minutes
Release Time: 10 minutes

1. To the Instant Pot, add the water, chili seasoning blend or chili powder, kidney beans, and pinto beans. Pour the tomatoes on top (do not stir). Add the frozen Bolognese sauce on top. Season with salt and add the bomba sauce, if using, for a spicy chili; do not stir.

2. Seal the Instant Pot and set to high pressure. Cook for 15 minutes; do a natural release of the steam pressure for 10 minutes. Stir the chili to combine. Ladle into bowls and top with crushed cheese bites or grated cheese.

INSTANT POT MUSHROOM RISOTTO

The constant stirring that risotto requires means it can be a pain on the stovetop. The Instant Pot comes to the rescue with the easiest risotto recipe ever.

1 (32-ounce) container Trader Joe's Hearty Vegetable Broth

1½ cups Trader Joe's Arborio Rice

1 tablespoon Trader Joe's Mushroom & Umami Seasoning Blend

¼ teaspoon kosher salt

1 (12-ounce) bag frozen Trader Joe's Mushroom Medley

½ cup Trader Joe's Parmesan, Romano, and Asiago Blend

1 tablespoon butter

Yield: 4 servings
Prep Time: 5 minutes
Cook Time: 5 minutes
Release Time: 15 minutes

1. To the Instant Pot, add the vegetable broth, arborio rice, seasoning blend, and salt. Add the frozen mushrooms on top.

2. Seal the Instant Pot and set to low pressure. Cook for 5 minutes; do a quick release of the steam pressure. Uncover and add the cheese and butter, stirring until the butter melts. Wait a few minutes for the mixture to thicken and then serve.

INSTANT POT SHRIMP ROLLS

Frozen shrimp is a dream to cook in the Instant Pot, and these Argentinian red shrimp from Trader Joe's are full of flavor. Note that even though they are pink, they're still raw, unlike most frozen shrimp.

1 cup water

1 (16-ounce) bag frozen Trader Joe's Argentinian Red Shrimp

2 tablespoons butter or vegan butter

kosher salt and freshly ground black pepper

¼ teaspoon Trader Joe's Everything But the Elote Seasoning Blend

Yield: 3 servings
Prep Time: 5 minutes
Cook Time: 1 minute
Release Time: 9 minutes

1. Place the trivet in the Instant Pot along with the water. Add the frozen shrimp to the Instant Pot on top of the trivet, if possible. Seal the Instant Pot and cook on high pressure for 1 minute; immediately do a quick release of the steam pressure. Remove the shrimp and let cool slightly. Roughly chop.

2. To a medium bowl, add the butter or vegan butter, and heat in the microwave until melted. Add the shrimp, stirring to toss. Season with salt, pepper, and the seasoning blend. Fill the hot dog buns with the shrimp mixture and serve immediately.

INSTANT POT CHICKEN SHAWARMA

Can't find pitas? Serve the Chicken Shawarma with Trader Joe's frozen jasmine or brown rice topped with a dollop of Trader Joe's Tzatziki.

1 cup water

1 package Trader Joe's Shawarma Chicken Thighs

2 Trader Joe's Pita Pockets

Trader Joe's Tzatziki, as needed

red onion slices, chopped lettuce, and diced tomatoes (optional)

Yield: 4 servings
Prep Time: 5 minutes
Cook Time: 12 minutes
Release Time: 15 minutes

1. To the Instant Pot, add the water and chicken thighs, including any seasoning liquid with the chicken. Seal the Instant Pot and cook on high pressure for 12 minutes; do a natural release of the steam pressure for at least 15 minutes.

2. Let the chicken cool slightly and roughly chop into pieces. Cut each pita into 2 pieces. Add as much tzatziki as desired to the pitas, and then fill the pitas with the chicken. Add the onion, lettuce, and tomatoes, if using.

INSTANT POT PULLED PORK BARBECUE SANDWICHES

Most pulled pork recipes call for huge chunks of pork. Although it has less marbling, pork tenderloin will work, and it will produce just enough pulled pork for a get-together.

1 Trader Joe's Peppercorn-Garlic Boneless Pork Tenderloin

¾ cup water

½ teaspoon kosher salt

¼ teaspoon freshly ground black pepper

1 cup Trader Joe's Carolina Gold Barbecue Sauce or any Trader Joe's Barbecue Sauce, divided

6 Trader Joe's Honey Wheat Hamburger Buns

Yield: 6 servings
Prep Time: 15 minutes
Cook Time: 50 minutes
Release Time: 30 minutes

1. Cut the pork tenderloin into 1-inch pieces. Add the pork to the Instant Pot, along with the water, salt, pepper, and ¼ cup of barbecue sauce. Seal the Instant Pot and set to high pressure. Cook for 50 minutes; do a natural release of the steam pressure for 30 minutes.

2. Using a slotted spoon, transfer the meat to a medium bowl. Let cool slightly and shred with tongs or 2 forks. Stir in the remaining ¾ cup of barbecue sauce, tasting and adding more barbecue sauce if needed. Serve on the hamburger buns.

EASY INSTANT POT HAMBURGER MAC and CHEESE

Box mac and cheese + frozen Bolognese is a match made in Instant Pot heaven.

1 (6-ounce) box Trader Joe's Organic Shells and White Cheddar, powdered cheese reserved

1 cup water

1 (12-ounce) package frozen Trader Joe's "Just Sauce" Turkey Bolognese

¼ teaspoon kosher salt

½ cup Trader Joe's Shredded Sharp Cheddar Cheese

Yield: 2 servings
Prep Time: 5 minutes
Cook Time: 4 minutes
Release Time: 14 minutes

1. To the Instant Pot, add just the shells from the mac and cheese box, reserving the cheese powder for later. Also add the water and place the frozen Bolognese sauce on top of the mixture. Season with the salt.

2. Seal the Instant Pot and set to high pressure. Cook for 4 minutes and then do an immediate quick release of the steam pressure. Stir in the reserved powdered cheese and shredded cheese. Let sit for a few minutes to thicken. Serve.

INSTANT POT SALSA CHICKEN

Use this easy chicken recipe to top rice and beans or mix into a salad.

1 Trader Joe's Organic Boneless Skinless Chicken (around 1½ pounds)

1 (12-ounce) jar Trader Joe's Salsa Verde or Trader Joe's Salsa Autentica

2 teaspoons chili powder

½ teaspoon kosher salt

Yield: 4 servings
Prep Time: 5 minutes
Cook Time: 12 minutes
Release Time: 15 minutes

1. To the Instant Pot, add the chicken, salsa, chili powder, and salt. Seal the Instant Pot and set to high pressure. Cook for 12 minutes; do a natural release of the steam pressure for 15 minutes.

2. Using a slotted spoon, transfer the meat to a medium bowl. Let cool slightly and shred with tongs or 2 forks.

CHAPTER 14

DESSERTS & DRINKS

A lot of people sail through dinner just to make it to the dessert. I mean, who doesn't enjoy indulging in a sweet treat? When I was in college, my desserts consisted of dry cakes from the dining hall or a tub of Ben & Jerry's. Baking just wasn't something I did. Thinking back, it's pretty inexcusable. These recipes will reward you with some easy sugary decadence. There are tons of delicious homemade desserts that don't require a ton of work, like Sunflower Seed Butter Cookies, made from just three ingredients. And while some recipes, like Raspberry Brownies, are a great way to treat yourself at the end of the day, others, like Banana Bread with Pralines, are good for impressing your friends with your crazy baking skills.

And let's not forget about drinks. For some college students, drinking is mainly associated with the least expensive alcohol available. But, you can make boozy drinks that taste downright delicious, like sangria made from Trader Joe's affordable wines or a chocolate milkshake spiked with Kahlúa.

ULTIMATE BERRY MUFFINS

These can double as a breakfast snack or end-of-the-day treat.

2 cups water

1 (8-ounce) bag Trader Joe's Dried Berry Medley

2 large eggs

⅓ cup vegetable oil

1 (18.25-ounce) box Trader Joe's Blueberry Muffin Mix or 1 (15.5-ounce) box Trader Joe's Triple Berry Bran Muffin Mix

Yield: 12 muffins
Prep Time: 15 minutes
Cook Time: 25 minutes

1. Preheat the oven to 350°F. Spray 12 muffin cups with cooking spray.

2. Fill a microwave-safe bowl with the water and microwave on high until the water boils, about 3 minutes. Add the dried berries to the water and let the berries soak for 10 minutes. Drain.

3. In a large bowl, use a fork or whisk to combine the eggs and oil. Add the blueberry muffin mix or the triple berry bran muffin mix, and stir until the batter is combined. Gently fold in the berries with a spatula.

4. Fill each prepared muffin cup three-quarters full with batter. Bake until the tops of the muffins are crispy and a toothpick or knife inserted into the center comes out clean, 22 to 25 minutes.

SUNFLOWER SEED BUTTER COOKIES

This cookie recipe is for those days when you crave fresh, homemade cookies with little fuss.

1 cup sugar

1 large egg

1 cup Trader Joe's Sunflower Seed Butter

Yield: 12 cookies
Prep Time: 10 minutes
Cook Time: 5 minutes

1. Preheat the oven to 350°F. Spray a rimmed baking sheet with cooking spray.

2. In a medium bowl, mix the sugar, egg, and sunflower seed butter.

3. Roll tablespoons of dough into balls and arrange the balls about 1 inch apart on the prepared baking sheet.

4. Bake until just golden, about 5 minutes. Remove the cookies from the baking sheet onto waxed paper and let cool.

MONKEY BREAD

Monkey bread is a Southern staple. Balls of dough are rolled in cinnamon and sugar and drizzled with butter.

4 to 5 pieces Trader Joe's English Toffee with Milk Chocolate

⅓ cup unsalted butter, melted

2 (17.5-ounce) containers Trader Joe's Jumbo Cinnamon Rolls with Vanilla Icing

Yield: 4 servings
Prep Time: 15 minutes
Cook Time: 25 minutes

1. Preheat the oven to 350°F.

2. Seal the toffee into a plastic bag and pound into crumbs.

3. Drizzle the bottom of an 8-inch round pan with half of the butter and half of the crumbled toffee.

4. Unroll the cinnamon rolls and reserve the icing. Divide each one in half, then roll the halves into balls. Line up the cinnamon balls snugly next to each other in the pan. If you use a smaller pan, you may need to layer the balls on top of each other, which is fine. Drizzle the remaining butter over them and sprinkle with the remaining toffee crumbles.

5. Bake until the bread is puffy and golden, about 25 minutes. Remove from the oven, and, if desired, drizzle the monkey bread with the reserved icing. Pull apart the bread pieces to serve.

RASPBERRY BROWNIES

These low-fat brownies swap out oil for applesauce for a still-indulgent treat.

1 cup light sour cream

¼ cup applesauce

1 (13.7-ounce) box Trader Joe's Reduced Guilt (Fat-Free) Brownies

½ cup Trader Joe's Raspberry Preserves

Yield: 4 to 6 servings
Prep Time: 10 minutes
Cook Time: 40 minutes

1. Preheat the oven to 350°F. Spray an 8-inch square pan with cooking spray.

2. In a large bowl, stir together the sour cream and applesauce. Add the brownie mix and stir until combined. Gently fold in the raspberry preserves with a spatula. Pour the batter into the prepared pan.

3. Bake until a knife or toothpick inserted into the center of the brownies comes out clean, 32 to 40 minutes.

VANILLA PUDDING CAKE

This cake is poked with holes once it comes out of the oven—that's not a mistake. The pudding topping is then poured over it to soak into the cake.

1 (16-ounce) box Trader Joe's Vanilla Cake and Baking Mix

1¾ cups milk, divided

½ cup vegetable oil

3 large eggs

2 tablespoons grated lemon zest, divided

1 (3.39-ounce) box Trader Joe's Instant Vanilla Pudding

Yield: 4 to 6 servings
Prep Time: 20 minutes
Cook Time: 60 minutes

1. Preheat the oven to 350°F. Spray an 8- or 9-inch round pan with cooking spray.

2. Pour the cake mix into a large bowl. Add ½ cup of milk and the oil, eggs, and 1 tablespoon of lemon zest. Mix the ingredients with a whisk until well combined. Pour the batter into the prepared pan.

3. Bake until the cake is golden and the center springs back when touched, 45 to 60 minutes.

4. In a microwave-safe dish, microwave the remaining 1¼ cups milk on high until warm, about 1½ minutes. Add the pudding mix, stirring until the pudding is thick. Stir in the remaining 1 tablespoon of lemon zest.

5. Using a knife or chopstick, poke 15 to 20 holes in the cake. Slowly pour the hot pudding over the cake so it fills the holes and is absorbed by the cake. Let cool.

BANANA BREAD with PRALINES

The addition of Trader Joe's Pecan Pralines really elevates this bread into the sublime.

2 bananas, cut into pieces

2 large eggs

⅓ cup unsalted butter, melted

¾ cup water

1 (15-ounce) box Trader Joe's Banana Bread Mix

1 cup chopped Trader Joe's Pecan Pralines or Trader Joe's Candied Pecans

Yield: 4 to 6 servings
Prep Time: 10 minutes
Cook Time: 60 minutes

1. Preheat the oven to 350°F. Spray a 9 x 5-inch loaf pan with cooking spray.

2. In a large bowl, mash the bananas with a fork.

3. In a medium bowl, whisk together the eggs, butter, and water. Pour the wet ingredients into the bananas, stirring to combine.

4. Add the banana bread mix to the wet ingredients and mix with a spatula until well combined. Fold in the pralines. Pour the batter into the prepared pan.

5. Bake until a toothpick or knife inserted into the center of the bread comes out clean, about 60 minutes.

GINGER ICEBOX CAKE

Icebox cakes are the easiest no-bake cakes ever.

1 tablespoon minced ginger

2 cups heavy cream, chilled

1 tablespoon sugar

2 (9-ounce) packages Trader Joe's Cookie Thins Triple Ginger cookies

Yield: 4 servings
Prep Time: 30 minutes active, plus overnight to set up
Cook Time: none

1. In a large bowl, place the ginger, cream, and sugar. Using an electric handheld mixer on high speed, beat the cream until stiff peaks form, 2 to 3 minutes, to make ginger-flavored whipped cream.

2. Set aside about one-fifth of the whipped cream and 6 cookies. On a large plate, use a spatula to gently spread about 2 tablespoons of the whipped cream to hold the bottom layer of cookies to the plate. Fit as many cookies as you can in a single layer on the plate.

3. On top of the cookies, spread a thin layer of whipped cream with a spatula. Repeat, adding another layer of cookies and whipped cream. Continue layering the cookies and whipped cream until you have 8 to 10 layers.

4. Use a spatula to cover the top and sides of the cake with the reserved whipped cream. Cover with plastic wrap and refrigerate for at least 8 hours.

5. When you're ready to serve the cake, seal the 6 reserved cookies into a plastic bag and pound into crumbles. Sprinkle the top of the cake with the crumbles.

DIRT DESSERT

This is a simple dessert that requires no actual baking and always draws rave reviews. It's a delicious, ultrarich chocolate mess.

1 (20-ounce) box Joe-Joe's Chocolate Sandwich Creme Cookies

3 cups milk

2 (4.09-ounce) boxes Trader Joe's Instant Chocolate Pudding

2 tablespoons unsalted butter, softened

8 ounces cream cheese, softened

1 cup powdered sugar

1 can sweetened light whipped cream

Yield: 10 servings
Prep Time: 30 minutes
Cook Time: none

1. Seal the cookies into a large plastic bag and pound to a sandlike consistency with a rolling pin or the bottom of a pan.

2. In a medium bowl, whisk together the milk and pudding mix until the pudding thickens. Set aside.

3. In a large bowl, place the butter, cream cheese, and sugar. Using an electric handheld mixer on low speed, cream the mixture until well combined and fluffy, 2 to 3 minutes. If you don't have a mixer, use a spoon, but make sure to mix it well. Using a spatula, fold the reserved chocolate pudding into the cream cheese mixture. Spray the whipped cream into the bowl and fold in to combine.

4. In a large serving bowl, spread one-third of the chocolate mixture, then one-third of the cookie crumbs. Repeat 2 times.

Note: The appearance of the top layer of cookie crumbs makes the dish look like a big bowl of dirt—if you want to get cute, you can place some gummy worms so that they look like they're crawling out of the top.

NUTTY CARAMEL POPCORN

In addition to giving you a very brief French lesson, the fleur de sel (artisanal salt) in the caramel sauce helps bring out the saltiness of the popcorn.

1 (3.2-ounce) packet Trader Joe's Microwave Popcorn with Natural Popcorn Flavor

3 tablespoons unsalted butter, melted

1 cup Trader Jacques' Fleur de Sel Caramel Sauce

1 cup Trader Joe's Roasted and Salted Mixed Nuts

Yield: 4 servings
Prep Time: 10 minutes
Cook Time: 5 minutes

1. Microwave the popcorn according to the package directions. Set aside.

2. In a large bowl, stir together the melted butter and caramel sauce to combine. Pour half of the popcorn into the bowl, along with the nuts. Stir to combine, making sure to coat all the popcorn with the caramel on the bottom of the bowl. Add the remaining popcorn and continue stirring to coat with the caramel.

3. Spread the popcorn mixture onto a baking sheet. Let sit for 5 to 10 minutes to slightly harden.

CHOCOLATE FONDUE

This fondue is so quick and easy to make using Trader Joe's chocolate syrup.

2 bananas

½ Trader Joe's Angel Food Cake

1 (1.2-ounce) package Trader Joe's Freeze Dried Strawberries

½ cup Trader Joe's Organic Midnight Moo Chocolate Flavored Syrup

½ cup semisweet chocolate chips, divided

Yield: 4 servings
Prep Time: 5 minutes
Cook Time: 2 minutes

1. Cut the bananas and the cake into bite-size pieces. Arrange them on a plate, along with the dried strawberries.

2. In a small microwave-safe bowl, stir together the chocolate syrup and ¼ cup chocolate chips. Microwave on high until melted, 1 to 1½ minutes.

3. Remove from the microwave and stir in the remaining ¼ cup chocolate chips.

4. Serve, dipping the fruit and cake pieces into the fondue. Reheat the fondue for 10 to 20 seconds in the microwave if it cools down.

SALTED CARAMEL SWIRLED BROWNIES

I'm biased, of course, but I think Trader Joe's makes the best brownie mix on the market. Add in a swirl of salted caramel for brownies everyone will swoon for. Also, coat the measuring cup with cooking spray when measuring the caramel sauce so it doesn't stick.

½ cup (1 stick) butter, melted

2 large eggs

1 (16-ounce) box Trader Joe's Brownie Truffle Baking Mix

2 ounces Trader Joe's Light Cream Cheese

¼ cup Trader Jacques' Fleur de Sel Caramel Sauce

Yield: 6 servings
Prep Time: 10 minutes
Cook Time: 45 minutes

1. Preheat the oven to 350°F. Spray an 8-inch square baking pan with cooking spray.

2. Let the melted butter cool slightly. Add to a large bowl with the eggs, whisking to combine. Add the brownie truffle baking mix and stir until combined. Pour the batter into the prepared pan, spreading so it's even.

3. Add the cream cheese to a small microwave-safe bowl. Heat just until soft, about 30 seconds. Stir in the caramel sauce. Add spoonfuls of the mixture on top of the brownie batter. Use a knife to swirl the caramel mixture and the brownie batter together the best you can (the brownie batter is thick).

4. Bake until a knife or toothpick inserted into the center of the brownies comes out clean, 35 to 45 minutes. Let cool completely before cutting to serve.

STRAWBERRY MOCHI CUPCAKES

The mochi cake mix brings a cool spongy texture to this twist on an American classic. Add the whipped cream right before serving.

1 (15-ounce) box Trader Joe's Mochi Cake Mix (a heaping 1½ cups)

1 cup room temperature water

2 large eggs

¼ cup canola oil

12 whole strawberries, hulled

1 can sweetened light whipped cream, as needed

¼ cup Trader Joe's Freeze-Dried Strawberries, crushed (optional)

Yield: 12 servings
Prep Time: 10 minutes
Cook Time: 30 minutes

1. Preheat the oven to 350°F. To a medium bowl, add the mochi cake mix, water, eggs, and oil. Stir until thoroughly combined.

2. Add 12 cupcake liners to a muffin tin. Distribute the batter between cupcake liners, filling them at least ¾ full. Carefully add a strawberry to each muffin batter, cut-side down. Bake until fully cooked, 25 to 30 minutes.

3. Let the cupcakes cool completely. To serve, top with the whipped cream and sprinkle with the freeze-dried strawberries, if using. Refrigerate leftovers for 1 to 2 days.

TWO-INGREDIENT BANANA ICE CREAM

For an extra spin on this two-ingredient ice cream, top with crushed Trader Joe's English Toffee.

2 bananas, peeled and sliced

¼ cup milk

Yield: 2 servings
Prep Time: 10 minutes
Cook Time: none

1. Add the banana pieces to a resealable plastic bag and freeze overnight.

2. To a blender or food processor, add the banana pieces. Blend, adding just enough milk to create an ice cream consistency. Serve immediately.

The I ♥ TRADER JOE'S® COLLEGE COOKBOOK

SPIKED CHOCOLATE MILKSHAKE

These milkshakes may look on the small side, but they're very rich.

1 cup Trader Joe's Ultra Chocolate Ice Cream

5 Joe-Joe's Chocolate Sandwich Creme Cookies (any variety), plus 2 for garnish

¾ cup Kahlúa, or other coffee liqueur

canned sweetened light whipped cream (optional)

Yield: 2 servings
Prep Time: 5 minutes

1. In a blender, place the ice cream, cookies, and Kahlúa. (Use more or less ice cream if you prefer a thicker or thinner shake.) Blend on high until combined.

2. Pour the milkshakes into 2 glasses. Top with whipped cream, if desired, and garnish with the remaining cookies crumbled on top.

BOURBON STREET SHAKE

Vanilla ice cream and bourbon meet a touch of salted caramel in this dreamy shake.

1 cup Trader Joe's French Vanilla Ice Cream

1 tablespoon Trader Jacques' Fleur de Sel Caramel Sauce

⅓ cup whole milk

⅓ cup bourbon

Yield: 2 servings
Prep Time: 5 minutes

1. In a blender, place the ice cream, caramel sauce, milk, and bourbon. (Use more or less ice cream if you prefer a thicker or thinner shake.) Blend on high until combined.

2. Pour the milkshakes into 2 glasses.

MICHELADA

This is a riff on the popular Tex-Mex version of a refreshing summer beer.

ice

2 tablespoons tomato juice

juice of 1 lime

½ teaspoon Trader Joe's
Jalapeño Pepper Hot Sauce, or
more

1 (12-ounce) bottle any Trader
Joe's lager

Yield: 1 serving
Prep Time: 5 minutes

1. Fill a large glass with ice.

2. Pour in the tomato juice, lime juice, and hot sauce, and stir to combine.

3. Slowly pour in the beer. Gently stir.

LOVE DRUNK PUNCH

The sparkling cider gives this punch an invigorating fizziness. Try not to make it too far in advance, as the carbonation will gradually fade.

½ (12-ounce) can frozen Trader
Joe's Organic Orange Juice,
thawed

2 cups Trader Joe's 100%
Pineapple Juice

1½ cups rum

½ cup peach liqueur

4 cups Trader Joe's Sparkling
Apple Cider

Yield: 6 to 8 servings
Prep Time: 5 minutes

1. In a large pitcher or bowl, place the orange juice, pineapple juice, rum, and peach liqueur. Stir or shake to combine, making sure the orange juice is dissolved.

2. Add the sparking apple cider, stirring more to combine.

SANGRIA

Sangria is a blend of wine, juice, and chunks of citrus or other fresh fruit.

1 (25-ounce) jar Trader Joe's Pear Halves in White Grape Juice
1 (750 mL) bottle any rosé or dry red wine
¼ cup triple sec
1 cup seltzer water
1 orange, cut into wedges
1 lemon, cut into wedges
1 bunch red grapes

Yield: 4 servings
Prep Time: 5 minutes, plus a few hours to chill

1. Chop the pears into small chunks and reserve the juice.

2. In a pitcher, stir together the grape juice from the pears, the wine, triple sec, and seltzer water.

3. Add the pear slices, orange wedges, lemon wedges, and grapes.

4. Refrigerate for a few hours until chilled.

GINGER BEER LEMONADE

If you haven't discovered the deliciousness that is ginger beer, available at Trader Joe's, then let this serve as an excuse to try it.

5 to 6 lemons
⅓ cup sugar
2 cups water
2 (12-ounce) bottles Trader Joe's Brew Ginger Beer

Yield: 4 servings
Prep Time: 5 minutes

1. Juice the lemons into a large pitcher.

2. Add the sugar, stirring to combine. Add the water, stirring to combine.

3. Top with the ginger beer, stirring to combine.

TIPS & TECHNIQUES

HOW TO PREPARE AN AVOCADO

Use a chef's knife to carefully cut the avocado lengthwise around the seed, cutting all the way through to the seed. Stab the seed with the knife, then twist and remove. To dice the avocado, take one half in your hand and use a paring knife to cut a crosshatch pattern into the avocado without going through to the peel. To slice, cut lengthwise. Use a large spoon and scoop out the avocado dice or slices.

HOW TO DICE AN ONION

1. Cut the onion in half vertically, straight through the root end and the stem end.
2. Peel both halves of the onion, discarding the peel.
3. Place the halves on a cutting board, cut-side down. Trim the stem ends.
4. Make numerous parallel cuts from the root end to the stem end, making sure to keep the root end intact. Cuts that are farther apart will result in larger dice; cuts closer together will yield smaller dice.
5. Carefully hold the onion at the root end. Make two or more even horizontal cuts, holding your knife parallel to the cutting board.
6. Holding the root end, slice crosswise, starting at the opposite end. The onion will fall into dice.

HOW TO BOIL AN EGG

If Trader Joe's is out of hard-cooked peeled eggs, or you just want to know how to make hard-cooked eggs on your own, here's what to do: In a medium pot, cover 6 to 8 large eggs with enough water to cover them. Bring the water to a boil over high heat. As soon as the water comes to a full rolling boil, cover the pot with a lid and remove it from the heat. Let the eggs sit in the hot water for 12 minutes. Carefully drain the hot water from the eggs. Fill the pot with cold water and ice cubes until the eggs have cooled enough to peel. For easiest and neatest peeling, do it as soon as possible.

HOW TO COOK AL DENTE PASTA

When cooking pasta, the goal is to boil it until it's al dente. But what exactly does that mean? An Italian phrase meaning "to the bite," al dente refers to the point when the pasta is cooked but still slightly firm to the bite. The best way to determine this is to taste the pasta as it cooks. Also, immediately after draining the pasta in a colander, make sure to toss it with a little olive oil. This prevents the pasta strands from sticking to each other and making a glop of noodles.

COOKING STEAK AND BURGERS

Keep in mind that the internal temperature of meat will rise by about 5 degrees while resting and that the following guidelines for beef account for that: for rare, 120° to 125°F; for medium-rare, 130° to 140°F; for medium, 145° to 150°F; for well-done, 155° to 165°F. The most accurate way to determine the doneness of steak is by using a meat thermometer, but you'll lose a bit of juice when the thermometer pokes a hole into the steak.

With a little of practice, you can learn to determine doneness by merely touching the steak with your finger—rare steak feels soft, with a lot of give; a tiny more give yields medium-rare; medium steak yields only slightly to the touch; and well-done steak feels hard to the touch. Resting is important because it allows the steak to finish cooking and retain its juiciness by redistributing its juices. If you cut into a steak without letting it rest, lots of delicious juices will escape.

IDEAS FOR LEFTOVER TRADER JOE'S INGREDIENTS

PESTO

- Whisk with vinegar and olive oil to make salad dressing.

- Mix with sour cream and dollop onto a baked potato or stir into mashed potatoes.

- Smear onto chicken, top with bread crumbs, and bake.

- Swirl into tomato soup.

- Beat into eggs before scrambling.

- Add 1 or 2 tablespoons to cooked rice, polenta, or grits.

- Dilute with oil and use as a marinade for meat.

- Layer onto a grilled cheese sandwich.

- Toss with ½ pound cooked Trader Joe's Italian Capellini pasta and Trader Joe's Grilled Lemon Pepper Chicken.

NUT BUTTER WITH BANANA SANDWICH

Wanna make this sandwich à la Elvis? Melt a little butter in a nonstick skillet over medium-high heat and sauté the assembled sandwich on each side until golden. Sprinkle with powdered sugar and serve.

PINE NUTS

Pine nuts are the edible seeds from certain varieties of pine trees. The small, almond-shaped nuts are actually located inside the pine cone. It's a time-consuming process to remove the nuts from the cones, which explains why pine nuts can be priced higher than other nuts. Add leftover pine nuts to any dish like soups, salads, and pastas when you want a touch of crunchiness.

RAW SHRIMP

Large, raw shrimp (peeled and deveined), like Trader Joe's Uncooked Wild Blue Shrimp, can be used instead of the cooked shrimp if you want a fresher taste. Thaw the shrimp, then cook as directed, increasing the time to 2 minutes.

CHILI

Use the leftover chili and queso dip to replace the chili and sour cream in a Frito Pie (page 31). Or, pour it over tortilla chips for nachos, or use it to top a burger.

CONVERSIONS

MEASURE	EQUIVALENT	METRIC
1 teaspoon		5.0 milliliters
1 tablespoon	3 teaspoons	14.8 milliliters
1 cup	16 tablespoons	236.8 milliliters
1 pint	2 cups	473.6 milliliters
1 quart	4 cups	947.2 milliliters
1 liter	4 cups + 3½ tablespoons	1000 milliliters
1 ounce (dry)	2 tablespoons	28.35 grams
1 pound	16 ounces	453.49 grams
2.21 pounds	35.3 ounces	1 kilogram
350°F / 400°F		175°C / 200°C

PHOTO CREDITS

RECIPE INDEX

ACKNOWLEDGMENTS

Thank you to all my friends and family who lent tons of encouragement—along with their stomachs to taste all the food—while I wrote the cookbook. Also, a big thanks to the ever-helpful staff at the NYC Trader Joe's locations.

ABOUT THE AUTHOR

ANDREA LYNN, author of *Fresh and Healthy DASH Diet Cooking* and *The Artisan Soda Workshop*, is a food writer and recipe developer based in Queens, NY. She has made a career out of highlighting grocery store ingredients and turning them into recipes, currently for *Savory* magazine. She has tasted almost every product Trader Joe's has on the market and can't control herself over the Candy Cane Joe-Joes.